AMERICAN CHRISTIANITY'S SLIDE INTO APOSTASY

Register This New Book

Benefits of Registering*

- ✓ FREE **replacements** of lost or damaged books
- ✓ FREE **audiobook** – *Pilgrim's Progress,* audiobook edition
- ✓ FREE information about new titles and other **freebies**

www.anekopress.com/new-book-registration

*See our website for requirements and limitations.

AMERICAN CHRISTIANITY'S SLIDE INTO APOSTASY

WHAT WE MUST DO BEFORE IT'S TOO LATE

Remember therefore from where
you have fallen; repent, and do
the works you did at first.
– Revelation 2:5

MICHAEL D. LEMAY

ANEKO
PRESS

We love hearing from our readers. Please contact us at www.anekopress.com/questions-comments with any questions, comments, or suggestions.

Visit Michael's website: www.michaeldlemay.com
American Christianity's Slide into Apostasy – Michael D. LeMay
Copyright © 2018

Scripture quotations are from the ESV® Bible (The Holy Bible, English Standard Version®), copyright © 2001 by Crossway, a publishing ministry of Good News Publishers. Used by permission. All rights reserved.

Cover Design: J. Martin
Cover Image: Helen's Photos/Shutterstock
eBook Icon: Icons Vector/Shutterstock
Editors: Sheila Wilkinson and Ruth Clark

Printed in the United States of America
Aneko Press
www.anekopress.com
Aneko Press, Life Sentence Publishing, and our logos are trademarks of
Life Sentence Publishing, Inc.
203 E. Birch Street
P.O. Box 652
Abbotsford, WI 54405
RELIGION / Blasphemy, Heresy & Apostasy
Paperback ISBN: 978-1-62245-102-9
eBook ISBN: 978-1-62245-103-6
10 9 8 7 6 5 4 3 2 1
Available where books are sold

Contents

Introduction

Words are important. More important is the definition we apply to those words. In today's increasingly confusing and hostile world, words like *love*, *tolerance*, and *bigot* are thrown around carelessly without clear definition, leading us to the brink of bitter divide and chaos. Our founders established this nation as "one nation under God," but we have morphed into a nation comprised of "red states" and "blue states" as the political divide in our nation threatens to tear us apart.

The Christian church in America has also fallen into the trap of carelessly using important words without clear, correct definitions. God gives specific definitions for words like *love*, *grace*, and *reconciliation* in His Word, but many professing Christians have redefined them because we value comfort over growth in our spiritual walk. God warns us of the importance of understanding and teaching His Word with the exact definitions He gives us:

> *Remind them of these things, and charge them before God not to quarrel about words, which does no good, but only ruins the hearers. Do your best to present yourself to God as one approved, a worker who has no need to be ashamed, rightly handling the word of truth. But avoid irreverent babble, for it will lead people into more and more ungodliness, and their talk will spread like gangrene. Among them are Hymenaeus and Philetus, who have swerved from the truth,*

saying that the resurrection has already happened. They are upsetting the faith of some. (2 Timothy 2:14-18)

God's Word uses specific words with exact definitions for our benefit. When we change His definitions to advance our own beliefs or agenda, He does not approve of our actions because, as these verses state, our changes ruin the hearers and upset the faith of some. Satan twisted God's warning to Adam and Eve about eating from the Tree of the Knowledge of Good and Evil. As a result of their disobedience, sin, decay, and death entered the world. Today, as some Christian churches twist the meaning of God's Word to facilitate their human agenda, they lead members away from God's definitions to more ungodliness and thereby undermine the faith, as the verses mentioned above warn.

This book is not an indictment of any particular denomination that professes Christianity. It is an indictment of American Christianity as a whole, which is infecting almost every denomination of practicing Christianity today. By my personal estimation, there are three distinct types of churches that claim to be Christian in our modern time:

- True Biblical Christianity churches (estimated 20 percent)

- Churches that have strayed into apostasy already (estimated 20 percent)

- Churches straying toward potential apostasy (estimated 60 percent)

The churches that have already succumbed to apostasy are probably beyond restoration; you should leave those churches immediately to save your eternal soul. Their teachings are often the exact opposite of what the Bible teaches, and their leaders know it, but they continue to advance their human agenda over God's. They are possibly the people God has turned over to a reprobate mind because they were taught the truth but consciously rejected it, as Paul describes in Romans 1.

The estimated 20 percent of churches which are Biblical Christian churches face increased pressure and persecution to conform to the world. We will discuss how this happens and how to battle against it.

The estimated 60 percent of churches that are being infected with American Christianity, which is the opposite of Biblical Christianity, can still be turned around and once again become Biblical churches. If the leadership that is being deceived is humble and willing to admit their error when the Word of God clearly points it out, the church can be restored to a truly Biblical church.

Always remember this: If your church is drifting from Biblical Christianity to American Christianity, your church leaders may not even realize it. In all probability they are not purposefully leading the church away from God and His Word. The subtle and dangerous deception Satan has mastered, along with ignorant but dedicated allies in public education, media, entertainment, and government, create a powerful yet subtle deception that is well masqueraded. Unless we are completely immersed and grounded in God's Word, we can easily be deceived into thinking we are serving God when in reality we are serving His enemy. That is how excellent Satan has become at his craft. One day Satan will be worshiped through his puppet, Antichrist, and many who worship him will be self-professed Christians.

We must understand how the father of lies and enemy of our souls has crafted his mastery of deception ever since he carried out his rebellion against God. He convinced Adam and Eve to walk away from an eternal life full of wonder and peace by convincing them to do the *one thing* God told them not to do. They could do anything they desired and eat from any tree except one, but Satan convinced them to eat from it anyway. He is so crafty and deceptive that he tempted Jesus in the wilderness by actually citing Scripture. But he used it out of context, and Jesus rebuked him with the complete context of God's Word. And over the past six thousand years he has finely tuned his craft of deception to the point that unless we are immersed in studying, understanding, and applying God's Word, we become easy targets for his trickery and deception. We can think we are serving and obeying God when in reality we are serving and obeying Satan himself.

After this I saw another angel coming down from heaven, having great authority, and the earth was made bright with his glory. And he called out with a mighty voice, "Fallen, fallen is Babylon the great! She has become a dwelling place for demons, a haunt for every unclean spirit, a haunt for

*every unclean bird, a haunt for every unclean and detestable
beast.*

*For all nations have drunk the wine of the passion of her
sexual immorality, and the kings of the earth have committed immorality with her, and the merchants of the earth have
grown rich from the power of her luxurious living."*

*Then I heard another voice from heaven saying, "Come out
of her, my people, lest you take part in her sins, lest you
share in her plagues; for her sins are heaped high as heaven,
and God has remembered her iniquities." (Revelation 18:1-5)*

Some who teach biblical prophecy believe Babylon represents the worldly
economic system. Some claim that New York City, the world's economic
center, is actually Babylon and that the attacks on 9/11 were a partial
fulfillment of these Scriptures. Others believe a renaissance will occur
in the city of Babylon itself, and it will again become the economic
capital of the world and the eventual throne of Antichrist when he rises
to power. This is short-sighted, human thinking.

In the Bible, Babylon represents everything evil that God warns us
about. Babylon is the epitome of human sin and rebellion against God.
It involves self-worship (the Tower of Babel), and wherever we read
about Babylon in the Bible, we see its effects: child sacrifice, human
pride, arrogance, sexual immorality, and fervent opposition to God's
people. Does that sound like any country you can think of? Why would
a Christian church partner with such a nation instead of speaking out
against its immoral behaviors and beliefs? But a growing number of
professing Christian churches are partnering with human government
in subtle but important ways that will eventually bring these churches
into slavery to a world government that bows to Satan.

Babylon represents the evil that will arise in these final days as an
unholy "marriage" between human government and religion. This is
one of the primary yet under-reported reasons that Martin Luther
started the Protestant Reformation. The Roman Catholic Church had
partnered with evil kings to promote their joint interest in power, control, and wealth. Adolph Hitler convinced the Catholic and Protestant

church leaders of his time to join him in his evil quest, convincing them that they both wanted the good of the German people. Within six months of their unholy alliance, he removed every Bible from the churches, and officials of Germany's Third Reich almost exclusively delivered the sermons.

America, the most powerful and influential nation in the history of the world, is repeating some of the same mistakes. As our nation slowly turns away from God and into the waiting arms of Antichrist, she looks more and more like Babylon every day. And American Christianity is forming another unholy alliance between human government and religion. In this book I will describe how American Christianity is falling into this trap by slowly aligning with a world that hates God. Many churches may not be conscious of where they are headed because the father of lies is cunning and deceitful, and he can make the worst of things appear to be good.

This is not a call to abandon assembling regularly as the body of Christ, and it is not a call to sit at home on Sundays to watch sports. It is certainly not a call for a new denomination within Christianity; I think twenty thousand denominations are quite enough. This book is a call to professing Christians to examine our beliefs and actions and to compare them to God's truth and standards in His Word. It is an attempt to help every professing Christian understand the deception perpetrated by the father of lies and that it infects both the secular and professing Christian institutions in our nation, such that in the final days one will not be able to distinguish between evil human government and religion. And it is a call for truly born-again, Spirit-filled Christians to spot deception and lovingly but firmly confront church leaders who are leading congregations away from true Biblical Christianity. These churches that are straying are not beyond restoration if leadership is humble and church members are courageous enough to confront leadership when it is clearly in error.

> *And I saw, coming out of the mouth of the dragon and out of the mouth of the beast and out of the mouth of the false prophet, three unclean spirits like frogs. For they are demonic spirits, performing signs, who go abroad to the*

kings of the whole world, to assemble them for battle on the great day of God the Almighty. (Revelation 16:13-14)

And I saw the beast and the kings of the earth with their armies gathered to make war against him who was sitting on the horse and against his army. And the beast was captured, and with it the false prophet who in its presence had done the signs by which he deceived those who had received the mark of the beast and those who worshiped its image. These two were thrown alive into the lake of fire that burns with sulfur. (Revelation 19:19-20)

And they marched up over the broad plain of the earth and surrounded the camp of the saints and the beloved city, but fire came down from heaven and consumed them, and the devil who had deceived them was thrown into the lake of fire and sulfur where the beast and the false prophet were, and they will be tormented day and night forever and ever. (Revelation 20:9-10)

We are foolish to ignore these clear prophetic warnings from God about a final unholy alliance between evil human government and a religion that supports and partners with it to oppose God one last time – spiritual Babylon. And it is clear that many professing Christian churches in America have already aligned with human government or will do so one day when pressure comes to bear.

Many verses in the New Testament where Jesus and the apostles warn of a "fake Christianity" that will grow in the days before our Lord's return inspired me to write this book. This fake Christianity is slowly abandoning the teachings of God in favor of the teachings of men. A dangerous cancer is infiltrating the American church, slowly eating away at its foundation. I believe this cancer has spread so wide that what we have come to know as "church" might well be beyond repair in many instances. This cancer does not discriminate; it is infecting every denomination of Christianity. At its root is the problem that started in the garden of Eden – the desire to elevate ourselves to God our Creator or perhaps even elevate ourselves *above* Him. We try to make God our servant, rather than the One we should serve with every breath.

I hope to make it abundantly clear in this book that there is a huge difference between a church that is *unaware* they are being seduced and pulled into American Christianity and a church that is *consciously* aware of its error in straying from God's Word. The former is a church that, if the leadership is humble, is able to correct its error and become what Jesus intends for His church. The latter is a church you should leave immediately; if you don't, in time you will probably become so immersed in a fake Christianity that your eternal soul may be in jeopardy.

Now the sceptic might question that last statement and invoke the "once saved, always saved" mantra. And while I do believe that once you are truly born again and receive God's Spirit you have eternal security, the question of "Can a person lose his salvation?" is not the best question we should ask as serious students of the Bible. The fundamental question we should ask is: "How can I know for sure I really *am* saved?" This gets to the root of the gospel of reconciliation, which we will discuss at length in this book. We will look at how the gospel increasingly presented today is really no gospel at all and is unable to save sinful man from the wrath of God. All it is doing is leading people into a false sense of security.

> *"Not everyone who says to me, 'Lord, Lord,' will enter the kingdom of heaven, but the one who does the will of my Father who is in heaven. On that day many will say to me, 'Lord, Lord, did we not prophesy in your name, and cast out demons in your name, and do many mighty works in your name?' And then will I declare to them, 'I never knew you; depart from me, you workers of lawlessness.'"* (Matthew 7:21-23)

This book is a call to *true* unity within the body of Christ and not the unity being advanced by some progressive movements in the church. Their unity is a house built on shifting sand that cannot stand up to the measure of truth. It sets aside the fundamentals of Biblical Christian faith and doctrine in favor of everyone getting along and resembles the attempts of building the Tower of Babel – an attempt to elevate man to the level of God.

In John 17 Jesus prayed that His disciples would be one as Jesus and God the Father are one. Jesus was one with the Father because they were in complete agreement on everything. He only said and did what the Father instructed. The unity we see being proposed in American Christianity today is the antithesis of the unity Jesus desired for His church. It is a conglomeration of contradicting beliefs based on the doctrines and desires of man instead of unity built on the rock of eternal truth we find only in God's Word.

> *"And I tell you, you are Peter, and on this rock I will build my church, and the gates of hell shall not prevail against it. I will give you the keys of the kingdom of heaven, and whatever you bind on earth shall be bound in heaven, and whatever you loose on earth shall be loosed in heaven."*
> (Matthew 16:18-19)

From these verses we know Jesus' true church will never be defeated no matter what the world or Satan throws at us.

> *If a kingdom is divided against itself, that kingdom cannot stand. And if a house is divided against itself, that house will not be able to stand.* (Mark 3:24-25)

Jesus spoke those words to expose the lie of the religious leaders who claimed His powers came from Satan. But the principle certainly applies to Christianity in America in these perilous times. Jesus established His everlasting church to spread the gospel of salvation and to develop a peculiar people dedicated to obeying His commands and glorifying God. But this "house" is being divided and rendered ineffective in its biblical purpose. Like an invasive cancer American Christianity has attached itself to the Biblical church, and it is eating away at the foundational health of the true church. We must identify and remove that cancer.

A skilled surgeon can often remove the cancer from a patient in a way that will not further harm the healthy part of the body so the patient can heal and return to a normal, productive life. The level of training and skill of the surgeon must be very high. Likewise, by the Word and Spirit of God, true believers can acquire the skills necessary to remove the cancer from a church and restore her to prominence and influence. But we must first acknowledge the existence of that cancer before it can be treated. The leadership of the church must be open to questions and critique and be humble enough to admit when God's Word proves they are in error.

Depart from me, you workers of lawlessness. These are the most chilling and ominous words our Lord and Savior ever spoke. And one day every man will stand before Him in judgment and perhaps hear these words that will condemn him to eternal punishment and separation from God. Surely Jesus was talking about those who are not Christians, and not about professing Christians. But taking a closer look.

> *"Enter by the narrow gate. For the gate is wide and the way is easy that leads to destruction, and those who enter by it are many. For the gate is narrow and the way is hard that leads to life, and **those who find it are few**."* (Matthew 7:13-14, emphasis added)

Few means exactly that – few. The word used is actually translated "a puny degree or number." Eighty percent of Americans still consider themselves Christians. Do you think 80 percent qualifies as "few"? Here is the question we need to consider: Do we want to trust our eternal destiny to anyone or anything except the Word of God? Do you trust your pastor or favorite television preacher with your eternal soul? Each person is responsible for his acceptance or rejection of the gospel. If you stand before Jesus on judgment day and are found guilty, claiming your pastor or televangelist misled you is no acceptable defense.

> *"Beware of false prophets, who come to you in sheep's clothing but inwardly are ravenous wolves. You will recognize them by their fruits. Are grapes gathered from thornbushes, or figs from thistles? So, every healthy tree bears good fruit, but the diseased tree bears bad fruit. A healthy tree cannot bear bad fruit, nor can a diseased tree bear good fruit. Every tree that does not bear good fruit is cut down and thrown into the fire. Thus you will recognize them by their fruits."* (Matthew 7:15-20)

Jesus warned us that many false prophets and teachers would deliver deception, but we should be able to recognize them!

I have spent the last nine years hosting a daily Christian radio talk show, *Stand Up For the Truth*. Our show looks at the news of the day and trends within the church; it points people to the eternal truth and wisdom of God's Word as the final say on all important matters. I have met and interviewed hundreds of pastors, ministry leaders, and Bible teachers, and I have talked with thousands of professing Christians. I have reached this conclusion: There is a distinct difference between Biblical Christianity and American Christianity. The first is based solely on the nature, character, and Word of God. The latter is built more and more on a secular foundation with worldly goals: popularity, wealth, and comfort. I documented much of this in my book *American Christianity's Adultery with Secular Culture* and its sequel, *The Death of Christian Thought: The Deception of Humanism and How to Protect Yourself.*[1]

American Christianity has far more in common with Babylon, the biblical example of self and pagan worship, than it does with Biblical Christianity. Any objective assessment of the trends and changing beliefs taught in many churches will confirm that American Christianity is on a fast track to becoming a major impetus behind the false one-world religion that God warns us about in both Daniel and Revelation.

Based on my study of the Bible, extensive research, and discussions with hundreds of self-professed believers and what they actually believe, there is a high probability that many professing Christians in America actually attend churches that could one day become a part of the apostate church that will fall away in the final days. I do not believe the pastors who lead these churches intend evil; they are simply falling for the lies of the enemy whose goal has been to discredit the church and diminish what Jesus created it to be – the light and salt to a world desperate for hope. Part of Satan's plan is to make the church look so similar to this world that there will be nothing to distinguish it from secular culture.

Having said that, in no way am I insinuating that all churches are this way. I know several solid Bible-teaching pastors who remain faithful to God's Word and are committed to shepherding the flock Jesus

---

1   Available from www.michaeldlemay.com

has assigned to them. But even those churches and pastors who are faithful at this time will be pressured in ways they cannot or will not imagine; it remains to be seen if they will succumb to the pressure of this fallen world or remain faithful to the very end. We will document in this book how the world is steadily bringing pressure on Christian churches to conform to itself or face dire consequences.

I have written about the worldly deceptions infiltrating American churches in my previous books, so I will not spend a great deal of time on them in this book, except to share the big picture of what is happening. The focus of this book is on the individual who professes to be a Christian and a follower of Jesus Christ. I hope to:

- Help you determine once and for all if you truly are a disciple of Jesus Christ or have fallen for the clever deception of fake Christianity addressed by Jesus in Matthew 7

- Help the committed believer stand firm against the deception of this world infiltrating the professing church at an alarming rate

- Help you determine if the church you attend is straying into American Christianity, abandoning the ways and teachings of God for its own human doctrines and understanding

- Help your church leaders see their error if the church is drifting into American Christianity

- Help the reader to bring wisdom into discussions with Christians over doctrinal differences and divisions that so easily pit Christian against Christian and prevent us from focusing on the lost while infighting like little children

One thing that inspired me to write this book is the growing illiteracy of the Word of God among professing Christians. Many of them hold personal views or beliefs that directly contradict God's Word. As secular society touts homosexuality, gender fluidity, and abortion, it is shocking how many professing Christians express support for these views while claiming they are born-again believers. This is important when we understand something very profound that Jesus said:

*The one who rejects me and does not receive my words has
a judge; the word that I have spoken will judge him on the
last day. For I have not spoken on my own authority, but the
Father who sent me has himself given me a commandment –
what to say and what to speak.* (John 12:48-49)

Jesus is the Word of God from Genesis 1 through Revelation 22. Jesus said that the Word of God will be used to judge all men when they stand before Him. One deceptive teaching that is creeping into American Christianity is that the Jesus of the New Testament somehow replaced all those commandments of God in the Old Testament. This has led to confusion and arguments on several fronts. It also contradicts the biblical teaching that God is perfect, non-contradictory, and never changing. If Jesus replaced and nullified the Old Testament teachings of God, then God is a liar and none of His Word can be trusted. This agrees with a common statement we hear from a growing number of progressive Christians, that the Bible, a two-thousand-year-old book, couldn't have anticipated issues like abortion and gender fluidity and therefore cannot be trusted. Instead, they teach that we must rely on our feelings and emotions (the flesh) to determine right from wrong. This undermines God's sovereignty and eternal perfection.

In addition to identifying the false and dangerous teachings infiltrating American Christianity, this book will equip the reader to be a strong biblical apologist; it will help professing Christians see the error of their beliefs and answer questions of a lost world in desperate need of hope. Sadly, biblical apologetics is becoming a lost art, but we need it more than ever as our nation and the church that is supposed to hold it accountable slip into spiritual disarray and cultural chaos.

There are no new biblical revelations in this book. God has given us everything we need in His Word. What is in this book is common sense and wisdom God gave true believers in His Word and through His Spirit, explained in a way that every serious Christian can understand and apply. God gave wisdom that allows the born-again believer to separate deception from truth, wisdom that allows us to understand both the basic and deeper teachings of God's Word, and wisdom to help those being deceived to come into the light of God's truth.

We will begin with an overview of how American Christianity is increasingly contradictory to Biblical Christianity. We will look at the subtle deceptions the enemy and his henchmen use to lead pastors and everyday Christians astray. Of utmost importance will be the discussion on how churches define success in these postmodern times. Is success a growth in "nickels and noses"? Or is it a growth in spiritual maturity of the church members?

We will then show how you can spot early warning signs that your church or denomination might be slipping into American Christianity and how you can determine if this is intentional or not. If it is unintentional, we will share how you can help your church's leaders right the ship and stay in the framework of Biblical Christianity. We will discuss when to submit to authority and when to respectfully confirm that we must obey God and not men.

We will look at how we can speak the truth in love and confront people in error for their benefit. How can we use truth *and* grace to help a Christian who is falling into a pattern of sin? What is the correct biblical way to judge others? We will discuss the importance of using God's definitions for the words He uses instead of redefining them to feed our flesh. We will discuss how a person's response when they are proven wrong exposes their true heart.

We will also discuss the rapid approach of persecution against born-again believers in our nation and how the world ramps up its attack plan from dismissal to ridicule, from ridicule to public silencing, and from public silencing to dictating what we can teach and learn in our very own churches.

We will lay out a foundation for what a true Christian church should look like according to the Bible. What is the structure and role of leadership? What are the roles of men and women, and husbands and wives within the body of Christ? We will contrast the world's definition of a successful church with the Bible's teachings. How does the Christian church equip members for the work of God in this dark world?

We will discuss how this fallen world has infiltrated not just American Christianity but even the hearts and minds of committed Christians. How do we guard our hearts and minds from clever deception that masquerades as truth? We will discuss how the world is bullying us and how our fear of confronting that bullying has led to the sad state of "secondary" bullying where Christians turn on one another out of pride. We make ourselves feel better as victims by bullying others, a sad testimony about the love or lack thereof within the body of Christ.

We will see how to apply the principles and teachings of God's Word in this book to become effective evangelists, biblical apologists, and leaders in our churches and communities. We will see how the peace and joy we exhibit can one day be an almost irresistible attraction to the lost as this world gives less and less hope.

We will understand the power of applying "Biblical Conjunctives" to answer important questions that confuse and divide Christians and render us ineffective for God's work. We will learn:

- How we can know for sure we are truly born-again believers instead of people being deceived by our own hearts

- How we can know if another person is truly a born-again believer or is being deceived by fake Christianity

- How to reconcile God's grace with God's law in a non-contradictory way

- How to determine if a false teacher or pastor is a deceiver with evil intent or is simply misled and capable of restoration through humility

- How to determine if a person is open to the gospel or has been turned over to a reprobate mind (Romans 1). When do we cast pearls or walk away?

- How we can show deceived professing Christians and unbelievers that they are in a state of contradiction in their stated beliefs and destroy their arguments and hopefully open their eyes to the truth – all by speaking the truth in love

It is time to make a clear distinction between Biblical Christianity and American Christianity and choose which church we will belong to and serve. Will we be taught and guided by God's Word or by the clever schemes of man? Satan's deceptive tactics are so powerful that he can convince us we are serving God when we are actually serving him and his evil agenda. If your church leaders see the error of their ways, they can consciously choose which type of church they want to lead – God's or man's. And you can decide whether to try to continue to influence the church you attend or leave it behind for a church that follows God and not men.

One important point I hope I make very clear in this book is this: Only God is completely right one hundred percent of the time. Every man and institution is some combination of right and wrong and no individual or church has perfect biblical doctrine. The church you currently belong to may indeed be slipping into American Christianity, but that does not mean your church leaders are consciously embracing this slide. Satan is so clever he'll try to convince us we are serving God when we are actually serving him. Your church leaders have earned the right to be confronted in their potential error with grace and respect if you see dangerous signs. If they are humble and true biblical leaders, they will listen, carefully consider, and then respond to your concerns. But if they double down on error when the Bible proves they are wrong, if they pull rank on you and bully you into silence and compliance, then leave that church as fast as you can because you are being conditioned to follow men, not God.

A critical goal of this book is to help you discern if the church you attend is straying away from Biblical Christianity into the arms of American Christianity. Our goal is to always help any church that is straying into American Christianity to correct its slide into apostasy and be restored to a Biblical Christian church. The key is to correctly identify if church leaders are conscious deceivers or simply deceived into thinking they are doing the right thing. Remember, most of these church leaders are not aware of their spiritual slide into apostasy, so we must approach this challenge biblically and systematically.

Step 1
Recognize only God is right all of the time. Every man or institution is some combination of right and wrong. The Bible is the only standard

that can distinguish between truth and clever deception from men or demons. Every one of us is susceptible to deception at some time.

Step 2
Understand that Satan is the father of lies and a master of deception. He is so devious and clever that he can appear as *an angel of light* (2 Corinthians 11:14). He is so deceptive that he convinced Adam and Eve to walk away from God's protection. He used Scripture out of context to tempt Jesus to sin, but Jesus rebuked him with Scripture in correct context. Satan and deceivers will misrepresent God's Word to deceive us.

Step 3
We must be able to accurately interpret God's Word (2 Timothy 2:15). We must first believe that the entire Bible from Genesis to Revelation is truth. It requires that we trust in God's eternal, unchanging nature and character. We attain a greater understanding and wisdom in God's Word when we embrace the principles God has given us in His Word. These are:

- Causality – cause and effect
- Non-contradiction
- Connections between freedoms and responsibilities or restrictions to those freedoms

We are then able to distinguish between opinions of men and truth from God.

Step 4
Understand there is an important biblical difference between *deceivers* and those who are *deceived*. A deceiver is one who knows the truth but teaches something to the contrary in order to deceive others for his benefit. Deceived people are not consciously aware they are being deceived. According to the Bible, people who are deceived should be dealt with gracefully and patiently. Deceivers should be called out, marked, and avoided. In Matthew 7:6 Jesus commands us to not throw our pearls before pigs because they will trample the pearls and turn

on us. Since He commands this, we should be able to identify "pigs" (conscious deceivers).

Step 5

The ultimate test to determine if a person is deceived or a conscious deceiver is whether the Holy Spirit or a different spirit is influencing the person. Born-again believers receive the Holy Spirit, whose role is to convict us of ongoing sins and testify to the truth of Jesus Christ (the Word of God). If we are under deception, the Holy Spirit will convict us of our wrong beliefs after we are confronted with them. Our conscience will be pricked when our wrong beliefs oppose the Spirit of God if we are humble when confronted in error through God's Word.

The person void of the Holy Spirit has a conscience so hardened against God that he will justify his beliefs and actions that contradict God's Word. As Paul wrote in 2 Timothy 3:13, they *go on from bad to worse, deceiving and being deceived.*

Step 6

If leaders who have been deceived see their error and repent, they should receive forgiveness and grace and be allowed the opportunity to correct the error in the church. But if they prove to be conscious deceivers, they must not be allowed to continue without consequences. Do not leave the church quietly for the sake of peace. Tell people why you are leaving, so the leader's deception can be recognized by all. The Purpose Driven Church model is built on intimidating and bullying into silence anyone who dares question the motives or teachings of American Christianity. Love people enough to be honest about the serious issues that cause you to leave.

One more crucial point will be addressed in this book. American Christianity is fraught with highly charismatic, charming men who have been groomed to be persuasive leaders. These are men of eloquence and charm who deliver their message with passion and conviction. Every Sunday people leave their churches inspired by such men instead of being inspired by God's Word. This is exactly what Satan wants! He wants you to be under the influence of men of charm, charisma, and persuasion, because the day is coming when the most inspiring and persuasive man ever born will be introduced to the world. He will inspire and challenge his followers; he will tell them they have the power to change this world for the better if they will just follow him, and many millions, including professing Christians, will follow him. The Bible calls him Antichrist.

The Pharisees of Jesus' time twisted God's law to the point that it became so convoluted that the Jews followed the Pharisees instead of God. They were so confused and ignorant of God's Word that they did not even recognize that Jesus was the Messiah they had been awaiting. They had been conditioned to follow men, not God. This exact thing is happening again in American Christianity. And once you have been thoroughly indoctrinated to follow a man instead of God, you are only one step away from following Antichrist, because his charm, charisma, and persuasiveness will dwarf those of the man you are currently following.

Chapter One

Babylon the Great: Distinguishing Biblical Christianity from American Christianity

Biblical scholars have debated for centuries the meaning of *Babylon* in Revelation. Some equate it to the actual city, which still modestly exists today; they claim it will be revived and rise to worldwide prominence once again. Others make a direct tie to Rome, which hosts the hierarchy of the Roman Catholic Church. Perhaps either of these could hold merit, but I believe they both miss the big picture. Babylon is more spiritual in nature than physical. If we focus on whether the role of the city of Babylon or the Roman Catholic Church as Babylon is intended, we divert our attention and efforts from what is most important – that the spirit of Babylon will rise to great heights in the final days, deceive many, and lead them to eternal destruction.

In the Old Testament, Babylon was the epitome of idolatry. The Tower of Babel was constructed so that man could ascend to the heavens and be like God – a sad replay of what took place in the garden of Eden.

But what exactly is idolatry? Most think of it as worshiping a false deity like the god of Islam or Mormonism, and while that is accurate, it is incomplete. The word Paul uses for *idolatry* in 1 Corinthians 10:14, where we are told to *flee from idolatry*, is *eidololatreia*, which means "image-worship." Man is the only creation of God made in His image.

So idolatry surpasses worshiping the false god of Islam, Mormonism, or any other false religion. It also encompasses *self-worship*.

In my role as host of a Christian radio talk show, I am often asked what I see as the greatest threat to Christianity in America. Is it Islam? The emergent church? New Age theology? The LGBTQ movement? While all of these could be considered threats, they are all simply effects of one cause and the results of something much larger and graver. The single greatest threat to Christianity in America is self-worship. It is manifested throughout movements like emergent theology, the New Age religion, and false teachings such as universal salvation. But the greatest threat is man's continuing attempts to elevate himself as god, which is subtly being implemented in many churches, perhaps even without the conscious knowledge of today's church leaders.

Whenever man is elevated and God is diminished, we are embracing the deception of Babylon. Several teachings and movements have crept into the professing American church that fit this model:

- Distortion of the nature and character of God in a way that contradicts God's own words

- Misrepresentation of the nature of fallen man

- Universal salvation theology

- The Church Growth Movement

- Dismissal of clearly spiritual issues as political

- Apathy toward the Old Testament

- Promotion of a false unity within the professing church

All of these dangerous infiltrations share a common root: the elevation of man's thoughts and ways over God's thoughts and ways. This is idolatry. They are based on the doctrines of secular humanism, a recognized religion that touts man as good and capable of getting better through his own evolution.

For nearly nine years, I have hosted *Stand Up For the Truth*. The reasons our board of directors started the show and what I have learned over the past eight years will bring the crisis that Christians face into focus. Our radio station, Q90 FM in Green Bay, Wisconsin, had been a primary sponsor of a large Christian music event in our area. But one day the festival organizers decided to invite a Marxist masquerading as a Christian to be its main speaker to talk to Christian youth about the need for social justice. Like most social justice warriors, Jim Wallis of Sojourners is a walking bag of contradictions who twists the Scriptures to fit his political agenda. While crying out for the church to support big-government programs aimed at eradicating poverty, immigration reform, and prison reform, he is strangely silent on the genocide of more than one million unborn babies every year; he also endorses such unbiblical tenets as homosexuality and gender fluidity. Wallis is a political operative and a historic Marxist who is emotionally and spiritually preying on young minds that are indoctrinated by government education and media, which detest the very thought of God. Yet here he was – invited with the enthusiastic blessing of the organizers of a Christian music fest to infiltrate the minds of naïve, professing Christians with his social justice rants.

This controversy birthed *Stand Up For the Truth*, and the Lord has blessed us with a worldwide audience as we look at the news and events of the world and bring them against the light of the Bible.

After a two-year hiatus from attending the annual music event, our radio ministry did go back and provided a booth; we worked with dozens of volunteers to share the gospel message with young people. I was in the midst of writing a book and decided to do an informal poll on what young people knew about God's Word and the gospel of salvation. I opened our discussions with youth who came to our booth with a simple question: "Are you a Christian?"

About 190 youth came to our booth, and all answered, "Yes, I'm a Christian." I asked how they knew they were Christians. All but three said, "Because Jesus died for my sins."

And then the big question: "Why did Jesus have to die a brutal death on the cross for your sins?" Only one could give the biblical answer – because of the righteous wrath of God against the sinful nature of man. Almost all the others admitted they did not know. This speaks profoundly to how the eternal nature and character of God are not being taught in many churches anymore. As we will see, an incorrect understanding of God's eternal nature makes it impossible to understand anything the Bible teaches.

A couple years ago, the same organization invited the singing group Gungor to appear at another event. Before the scheduled appearance, Michael Gungor publicly denied the Bible as truth and claimed he could no more believe in a literal Adam and Eve than he could the Easter bunny. We once again stood up and publicly questioned what was going on with the organizers, and this time the appearance was cancelled.

We might be tempted to simply dismiss these events as a single Christian ministry gone off the rails, but in reality it is a microcosm of what is happening in American Christianity. The gospel is being diminished, the Word of God plays second fiddle to celebrity pastors with egos and agendas, and entertainment has become the main attraction of many churches. If a church can offer cool music along with comfy chairs and a wonderful coffee bar, people will flock to that church.

And with a little luck, maybe the pastor will become the next celebrity with thousands of lukewarm Christians and an enormous budget to fund anything. Maybe he can get that elegant home or corporate jet that all the prosperity preachers get these days! But the pastor must make sure church doesn't disrupt the lives of the members by challenging their beliefs or actions. He will need to give them some milk so they will not starve, but not enough meat where they will actually grow strong in the faith, keeping them dependent so they will never question what is preached.

Stand Up For the Truth Radio

When we started our daily talk show in 2010, our goal was to alert the church of false teachings and dangerous movements that were seeking to infiltrate her. Little did I know at the time that we were a few years too late. The enemy had already planted spies and seeds in many churches with many of them abandoning biblical teachings for human wisdom. Many churches had aligned with deceptive programs and doctrines such as the Church Growth Movement, Word of Faith prosperity gospel, or emergent church doctrines that sacrificed individual spiritual growth for safe, seeker-friendly comfort. Some local pastors told church members to not listen to our show and claimed we were dividing the body of Christ. Deep down they realized that if church members checked everything taught from the pulpit against God's Word, questions and serious concerns would arise.

Many pastors who had been friends for years suddenly avoided me any way they could. They would call me occasionally and complain that I was being too hard on the church. I listened with a real desire to make sure I was being fair and accurate, but from many of these conversations I found that some of the men leading our churches could not explain basic doctrines of the Christian faith. They struggled with simple but important questions like explaining the full gospel or how Christians reconcile the law with grace or the rudimentary basics of biblical prophecy.

What started out as a hopeful call to the American church to purge false teachings and secular movements from its midst and equip church members to share the gospel and serve the body of Christ, has become a warning to professing Christians to leave American Christianity (Babylon) so their very souls might be spared. What I failed to understand at the time was this: I thought the church was *facing* problems, but I now realize that American Christianity *is* the problem! Just look at a few of the headline issues from the past few months we have covered on air:

- "Is God male? The Episcopal church considers changing its *Book of Common Prayer*."

- Pastor Bill Hybels and the entire Willow Creek board of elders resign over sexual scandal and cover-up.

- Pastor Andy Stanley tells his church members to "unhitch" from the Old Testament, claiming Jesus and Paul encouraged the same thing.

- *The Shack* author claims people get a second chance at forgiveness after death.

- More than half of all professing Christians believe God is okay with homosexuality.

- Three hundred Catholic Church priests in Pennsylvania abuse one thousand children and the diocese covers it up.

I am a fan of the movie *Braveheart* about Scotland's fight for freedom from the tyranny of England under King Longshanks. William Wallace, a commoner, rallies the Scots to overthrow the evil English kingdom's wicked rule but realizes he needs the Scottish nobles behind them. These Scottish nobles had been bribed by Longshanks for decades with land and titles, but Wallace finally thinks he has convinced Robert the Bruce, the most powerful Scottish noble, to join him in his fight for Scotland's freedom. The battle army is assembled and Wallace attacks – only to find out that the English army has set a trap and Wallace's troops are routed. Wallace is chased down by an enemy knight and seriously wounded without seeing the face of his attacker. Thinking Wallace has been killed, the enemy gets off his horse to turn Wallace's body over and finds him still alive. Wallace surprises the attacker by pulling a knife on him; he attacks and unmasks his enemy and discovers Robert the Bruce, the very man who pledged to fight with him. The look on Wallace's face as he sees he has been betrayed by a close ally is one of confusion and shock.

Many committed Christians believe in the American church. We fight for her by exposing enemies infiltrating her camp. We defend her against the attacks of secular humanists and society, but many of us have come to realize that the very institution we have been fighting to defend, American Christianity, has sold out to the enemy. American Christianity has become so contradictory to God's teachings that every serious Christian needs to decide if they will be members of a Biblical Christian church or choose to continue to belong to a church that is increasingly selling out to the world with each passing day.

First of all, I am not saying every church or denomination has sold out to American Christianity.

Second, I am not encouraging you to quit attending church. As disciples of Jesus Christ, we need Christian fellowship.

I only hope to help you distinguish between American Christianity and true Biblical Christianity. If the church you attend has fallen into the traps we discuss in this book, try to meet with your pastor and elders;

respectfully ask them questions and share your concerns. This will help you determine whether your church leadership is simply being misled or if it is intentionally leading the church down the wrong path. The humble leadership team will listen to your concerns and answer your questions. The prideful ones will dismiss you and perhaps accuse you of being an instigator. If this is the case, and you have been thoughtful and respectful in your discussions, then it is time to find a fellowship serious about following Christ instead of man.

Some important issues we will discuss in this book I have covered more extensively in my previous books, but they are important to grasp if we hope to understand deception from truth and become Biblical Christians.

Forgetting How to Think

The most important thing a serious Christian can master is this: how to distinguish between opinions, deception, lies, and truth. This is particularly important when we understand that the agenda of this world is to diminish your ability to think rationally, making you susceptible to diversion and deception on a myriad of issues. When people cannot think rationally and logically, they can be easily manipulated and controlled. Classical education, where children are thought *how* to think, has been replaced by indoctrination where they are taught *what* to think. The diminishing ability of the average American to think rationally and logically makes us ripe for deception.

An Inaccurate Perception of Reality

The infatuation with social media many people have is also diminishing our ability to think and maintain correct perspective. A recent story we covered on our radio show discussed the enormous growth in the numbers of young people having radical plastic surgery. Why? Because their selfies on social media, which can be filtered and doctored to make us look much younger and more attractive, are leading to depression when they look in the mirror and see they look little like what their selfies represent to others.

Studies show that as violent video games and virtual reality become the norm for more and more young people, their ability to distinguish reality from fantasy is leading to all sorts of psychological and emotional issues.

This inaccurate perception of reality is manifesting itself in American Christianity as we diminish the nature of God and man and diminish the true gospel. When we see God as less than He really is and see ourselves as better than we really are, the gulf between a perfect God and sinful man is presented as smaller, diminishing the gospel of salvation and the price Jesus paid for our ransom. The journey to forgiveness and salvation becomes a simple one-step journey of man instead of a sovereign, righteous, just, and holy God performing the greatest act of love and forgiveness the world will ever see, without compromising His nature and character.

Distinguishing between Opinions, Deception, Lies, and Truth

In the late 1960s, as the Vietnam War was costing thousands of American lives, journalism took a bold step that would forever change how Americans consume and comprehend news. Walter Cronkite, the famous CBS journalist who hosted the nightly news, started mixing commentary with factual reporting. The Federal Communications Commission ("FCC") first insisted that Cronkite distinguish between reporting facts and offering his opinions on those facts with a disclaimer. But the damage had been done. Journalism had crossed the line from reporting facts to indoctrinating people with a poor thought process by mixing and confusing facts with opinions. Today it is almost impossible to find a source on television or the Internet that only reports the news. Instead, we have a conglomeration of fact and opinion, and when combined with a diminishing ability to think rationally and logically, Americans are becoming indoctrinated in astounding ways.

One of the ways I teach people to use rational thought is to state a belief or opinion and then have them try to prove to themselves that they are wrong, instead of compiling facts and feelings to support their initial belief. I call this "contrastive thought" and it is used often in the

Bible. Paul's teachings in particular are very contrastive, particularly in the book of Romans where he reconciles God's law and grace.

But thinking contrastively requires humility and the recognition that we are not always automatically right in our opinions. Contrastive thought requires a desire for growth over comfort, something that goes against our sinful human nature and pride.

Freedom and Responsibilities

The current hot-button issue among NFL fans is some players protesting during the playing of our national anthem, choosing to take a knee to protest what they perceive to be injustices in our nation. President Trump, as he often does, has fanned the flames of social discourse by suggesting that NFL owners fire players who choose to protest. The two greatest false teachings confronted in the first-century church were the Judaizers and the Gnostics. The Judaizers were all about adding rules and restrictions to salvation, believing men were still bound by Judaism and the law as essential ingredients of salvation. The Gnostics believed in the freedoms Paul taught in Biblical Christianity but rejected the biblical restrictions and boundaries to those freedoms. By applying what I call biblical conjunctives to problems, you can discern between clever deception and truth. In the case of the NFL protestors the conjunctive is quite simple:

> **Freedom:** The constitution gives citizens the right to peacefully protest.

> **Restriction:** Courts have ruled that employees can be held accountable by employers for their conduct *while acting as employees.* This means if the employer does not want employees protesting on work time, they can be disciplined or fired for doing so.

> **Conjunctive:** Players are free to protest on their own time but not on company time if their employer tells them not to.

Every major doctrine and teaching in the Bible can be correctly understood using conjunctives. But the legalist focuses solely on the restrictions of the Bible while the Gnostic (emergent) focuses only on the freedoms. The Biblical Christian finds truth where these restrictions and freedoms intersect in God's Word.

So the keys to distinguish between Biblical Christianity and deceptive American Christianity are:

- Using rational, logical thought

- Having an accurate perception of who God is and who we are

- Distinguishing between opinions, deception, lies, and truth

- Using biblical conjunctives to discern between clever deception and biblical truth

The real key to implementing these tools is an understanding of how to correctly interpret the Bible. These will be recurring themes throughout this book. While we will touch base on the basics of these principles, the best way to study them in greater depth is to pick up a copy my book, *The Death of Christian Thought*.

The fundamental reason American Christianity is straying from Biblical Christianity is a wrong belief system regarding the character and nature of God and understanding the depths to which sinful man has fallen. If you do not get God's nature and character right, it is almost impossible to get anything else right since God created and sustains all things. Also, misunderstanding God's nature and character leads to deception and heresy surrounding the most important thing God has ever done: reaching down to sinful man with the gospel of salvation.

Presenting the Nature and Character of God in a Way That Contradicts God's Own Word and Misrepresenting the Nature of Fallen Man

If we do not understand God's nature and character, we cannot possibly get anything right, particularly the nature and future of man. God is the Creator and has existed for eternity. No one created God. God is Spirit and He manifested Himself in the flesh: Jesus Christ. Jesus is not separate from God; He is God Himself who came in the flesh to be the sacrifice for our sins upon the cross.

God's Nature and Characteristics

God Is Always Righteous

From the ends of the earth we hear songs of praise, of glory to the Righteous One. (Isaiah 24:16)

Henceforth there is laid up for me the crown of righteousness, which the Lord, the righteous judge, will award to me on that day, and not only to me but also to all who have loved his appearing. (2 Timothy 4:8)

God is a righteous judge, and a God who feels indignation every day. If a man does not repent, God will whet his sword; he has bent and readied his bow. (Psalm 7:11-12)

For the LORD is righteous; he loves righteous deeds; the upright shall behold his face. (Psalm 11:7)

If you know that he is righteous, you may be sure that everyone who practices righteousness has been born of him. (1 John 2:29)

This is by no means an exhaustive list of the Scriptures that show God's nature is always righteous.

God Is Just

"For I am with you to save you, declares the LORD; I will make a full end of all the nations among whom I scattered you, but of you I will not make a full end. I will discipline you in just measure, and I will by no means leave you unpunished." (Jeremiah 30:11)

"Yet you say, 'The way of the Lord is not just.' Hear now, O house of Israel: Is my way not just? Is it not your ways that are not just? When a righteous person turns away from his righteousness and does injustice, he shall die for it; for the injustice that he has done he shall die. Again, when a wicked person turns away from the wickedness he has committed

and does what is just and right, he shall save his life."
(Ezekiel 18:25-27)

"I can do nothing on my own. As I hear, I judge, and my judgment is just, because I seek not my own will but the will of him who sent me." (John 5:30)

If we confess our sins, he is faithful and just to forgive us our sins and to cleanse us from all unrighteousness. (1 John 1:9)

And they sing the song of Moses, the servant of God, and the song of the Lamb, saying, "Great and amazing are your deeds, O Lord God the Almighty! Just and true are your ways, O King of the nations!" (Revelation 15:3)

And I heard the angel in charge of the waters say, "Just are you, O Holy One, who is and who was, for you brought these judgments. For they have shed the blood of saints and proph-ets, and you have given them blood to drink. It is what they deserve!" (Revelation 16:5-6)

After this I heard what seemed to be the loud voice of a great multitude in heaven, crying out, "Hallelujah! Salvation and glory and power belong to our God, for his judgments are true and just; for he has judged the great prostitute who cor-rupted the earth with her immorality, and has avenged on her the blood of his servants." (Revelation 19:1-2)

God's nature (who He is) is always righteous and just, which makes Him holy (set apart; of one substance). His actions and behaviors are consistent with His nature, and He does not contradict Himself or lie. If God were not always righteous and just, He would not be a perfect God, and man would be left to arbitrary means of judgment, salvation, and righteousness, which is secular humanism.

Who Is Man before God's Saving Grace?

The Bible says much about the nature and character of sinful man, and it isn't very flattering. Things started out well, as man was to be the crown jewel of God's creation and take over all the earth (stewardship).

> *So God created man in his own image, in the image of God he created him; male and female he created them. And God blessed them. And God said to them, "Be fruitful and multiply and fill the earth and subdue it, and have dominion over the fish of the sea and over the birds of the heavens and over every living thing that moves on the earth." (Genesis 1:27-28)*

God desired that men would love and glorify Him by managing His creation, being fruitful, and multiplying His family. But love must be a choice, not forced upon another. So God gave man a free will to choose to love and obey Him or to reject Him. Man chose to know right from wrong, succumbing to Satan's seduction to eat from the Tree of the Knowledge of Good and Evil. Sin entered the world and man was separated from fellowship with God. God had to punish man for his sin, so man was expelled from Eden, and his intimate fellowship with God was damaged and quickly deteriorated over the centuries as he constantly chose disobedience over loving God. As man grew more and more sinful, God got to the point where He regretted creating him.

> *The LORD saw that the wickedness of man was great in the earth, and that every intention of the thoughts of his heart was only evil continually. And the LORD regretted that he had made man on the earth, and it grieved him to his heart. So the LORD said, "I will blot out man whom I have created from the face of the land, man and animals and creeping things and birds of the heavens, for I am sorry that I have made them." But Noah found favor in the eyes of the LORD.* (Genesis 6:5-8)

Man had been exposed to sin, and like a cancer, it continued to consume him.

> *And Moses said to Aaron, "What did this people do to you that you have brought such a great sin upon them?" And Aaron said, "Let not the anger of my lord burn hot. You know the people, that they are set on evil. For they*

said to me, 'Make us gods who shall go before us. As for
this Moses, the man who brought us up out of the land of
Egypt, we do not know what has become of him.' So I said
to them, 'Let any who have gold take it off.' So they gave it
to me, and I threw it into the fire, and out came this calf."
(Exodus 32:21-24)

Surely there is not a righteous man on earth who does good
and never sins. (Ecclesiastes 7:20)

The heart is deceitful above all things, and desperately sick;
who can understand it? "I the LORD search the heart and test
the mind, to give every man according to his ways, according
to the fruit of his deeds." (Jeremiah 17:9-10)

The picture is clear. Before receiving the grace of God, man is wicked
and depraved, compared to the righteousness of God. Since there was
no way man could be righteous enough to be pleasing and acceptable to
God, the source of this salvation had to be from God alone. However,
the responsibility for the success of this plan depended on man's willingness to admit he is wicked, evil, and incapable of doing anything about
it in his own strength, and to repent accordingly. He needs humility.
Once a man confesses and repents, asking God to direct his life moving
forward, he receives forgiveness and salvation from God.

The Gospel of Salvation

Now after John was arrested, Jesus came into Galilee, pro-
claiming the gospel of God, and saying, "The time is fulfilled,
and the kingdom of God is at hand; repent and believe in the
gospel." (Mark 1:14-15)

For I am not ashamed of the gospel, for it is the power of
God for salvation to everyone who believes, to the Jew first
and also to the Greek. For in it the righteousness of God is
revealed from faith for faith, as it is written, "The righteous
shall live by faith." (Romans 1:16-17)

The complete gospel message preached by Jesus Christ is the only way sinful man can be justified by God and have a right relationship with Him once again. Sadly, these days the true gospel has often been replaced with an "invite Jesus into your heart" message that is no gospel at all. It lacks the necessary ingredients given by the Bible for man to be forgiven of his sins and have a right relationship with God.

The gospel of salvation has four crucial components:

- **Heartfelt confession:** A person must sincerely admit he is a hopeless, helpless sinner deserving of God's wrath and punishment.

- **Heartfelt repentance:** The Bible's definition of repentance is "a change of mind that leads to a consistent change of behavior over time." Man must think differently about the sins he once enjoyed and justified. He must grow to hate his sin and realize the offense of his sins against a righteous and just God.

- **Complete faith and trust in Jesus Christ alone:** A man must place his complete intellectual and emotional faith in who Jesus Christ is (God in the flesh) and what He accomplished on the cross (He took the wrath of a just God upon Himself in our place). We recognize it is only by God's grace, granted to us through our confession, repentance, and complete faith in Jesus alone, that we are justified by God and brought back into a righteous relationship with Him.

- **Submitting to the lordship of Jesus Christ over all our lives:** This does *not* mean perfect obedience at all times. It *does* mean acknowledging Jesus as Lord and judge over all things and desiring, by the power of God's grace and Spirit, to be continually transformed into the image of Jesus Christ. Increasingly, as we live our lives, our desire is to be more like Jesus in thought, word, and deed.

Who Is Man after Salvation and Being Born Again?

The simple answer from the Scriptures is that we are a new creation as the result of being saved through spiritual rebirth.

> *Therefore, if anyone is in Christ, he is a new creation. The old has passed away; behold, the new has come. All this is from God, who through Christ reconciled us to himself and gave us the ministry of reconciliation.* (2 Corinthians 5:17-18)

The word *reconciliation* means "to be restored; atoned for." It means man returns to the state he was in when God created him: correct spiritual alignment with his Creator. We recognize God is right and we were wrong. There is no compromise involved; it is a total surrender to the righteousness and justice of God. How can we know we have been reconciled?

> *Remind them of these things, and charge them before God not to quarrel about words, which does no good, but only ruins the hearers. Do your best to present yourself to God as one approved, a worker who has no need to be ashamed, rightly handling the word of truth. But avoid irreverent babble, for it will lead people into more and more ungodliness.* (2 Timothy 2:14-16)

The born-again believer is a new creation, now able to throw off the chains of sin and wrong beliefs that previously made us slaves to sin. We are able to now take our thoughts captive in obedience to Christ and free ourselves from wrong beliefs and lies we had accepted previously as truth. We are a work in progress, being continually sanctified by God for His glory and our benefit both in this life and for eternity.

The onslaught of secular humanism that is infiltrating American Christianity is only possible when professing Christians do not understand the biblical narrative on God's nature and character along with man's inherent sinfulness and wickedness. When that becomes perverted, everything is open to an attack of deception. Of utmost importance is understanding the nature and character of God along with understanding this: Sinful, fallen man is the exact opposite of God! We are everything He is not: prideful, rebellious, sinful, lovers of self, etc. To see this truth in a lesser light is to believe that man can save himself through "growth." To be reconciled to God means that by His grace we are now in agreement with Him. And that means we never question His Word or try to put our own human slant on it. As the verses in 2 Timothy above state, we are approved by God when we rightly handle His Word: the eternal Bread of Life.

The American Christianity View

What is being increasingly taught in our churches contradicts what the Bible says about God and man's nature and what reconciliation looks like.

The Nature and Character of God in American Christianity

God's righteousness and justice is being downplayed or eliminated from many churches. The call to unhitch from the Old Testament teachings is fueling this exodus from biblical knowledge and understanding. We will hear the love part of God's nature emphasized, but at the expense of truth.

How many times do we hear unbelievers say, "A loving God would never send anyone to hell"? Worse yet, we hear that heresy coming from the mouths of more professing Christians and pastors regularly. It's like they believe somehow Jesus replaced the Old Testament God who spoke of wrath against sin and hatred for the unrepentant sinner. That somehow God just decided to change His nature and overlook sin, now deeming it as acceptable in His eyes.

> *God is not man, that he should lie, or a son of man, that he should change his mind. Has he said, and will he not do it? Or has he spoken, and will he not fulfill it?* (Numbers 23:19)

> *"For I the LORD do not change; therefore you, O children of Jacob, are not consumed."* (Malachi 3:6)

> *Do not be deceived, my beloved brothers. Every good gift and every perfect gift is from above, coming down from the Father of lights, with whom there is no variation or shadow due to change. Of his own will he brought us forth by the*

word of truth, that we should be a kind of first fruits of his creatures. (James 1:16-18)

So when God desired to show more convincingly to the heirs of the promise the unchangeable character of his purpose, he guaranteed it with an oath, so that by two unchangeable things, in which it is impossible for God to lie, we who have fled for refuge might have strong encouragement to hold fast to the hope set before us. We have this as a sure and stead-fast anchor of the soul, a hope that enters into the inner place behind the curtain, where Jesus has gone as a forerun-ner on our behalf, having become a high priest forever after the order of Melchizedek. (Hebrews 6:17-20)

The problem facing American Christianity is that it cannot reconcile God's righteous and just nature with His love, grace, and mercy. To them it is either one or the other: He is *either* righteous and just *or* He is loving and merciful. This is simply sloppy hermeneutics brought forth from a heart of humanism: the belief that man is actually good in his nature.

The Nature of Man in American Christianity

We saw that the Word of God paints a very unflattering picture of the nature of man. Man is by his sinful nature wicked and evil, incapable of any lasting good. Oh, he may be capable at times of doing some-thing righteous, but even that is tainted with the motive of self-interest. American Christianity has adopted the beliefs of secular humanism that man is at his core good, and applies it to the gospel, in essence preaching a false gospel of reconciliation.

Who Is Being Reconciled to Whom?

The word *reconciliation* is defined by the Bible as "to be restored and atoned for." Biblical reconciliation is sinful man being atoned for by the sacrifice of the spotless Lamb of God (God in the flesh) and being restored to his state before sin entered the world. American Christianity has become more like this: somehow reconciling the bridge between God and man through compromise and God meeting us halfway. In other words, we give some and God gives some. We want to go to heaven so God compromises on His righteous and just nature. We become more like God and He gives in and becomes more like us. This is flat-out apostasy, yet it is what is, perhaps unconsciously, being presented in many churches as the "gospel" these days.

"Just invite Jesus into your heart." That is nowhere in the Bible and falls far short of the gospel. The gospel begins with man surrendering to God, not seeking compromise with Him. We acknowledge God is eternally right, just, and perfect; and we are hopelessly sinful and incapable of change on our own. But if you listen carefully to both what is being taught and *not* being taught in many churches, you will see this compromise of the gospel being presented regularly.

Here is a chart that differentiates how Biblical Christianity and American Christianity view and teach the reconciliation of the gospel:

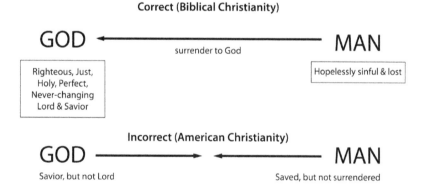

Gospel of Reconciliation

This false reconciliation is leading to another dangerous theology infiltrating the church through men like Brian McLaren, Rob Bell, William Paul Young, and others.

Universal Salvation

"How could a loving God ever send anyone to eternal hell?" American Christianity always asks the wrong questions. The correct question is this: "How could a perfect, sinless, righteous, just, and holy God ever allow *anyone* into heaven?" The first question speaks to our pride and lack of understanding of God's Word. The second question is a realization of our sinful, rebellious nature against God and a recognition of how a perfect God reconciles righteousness and mercy.

The true disciple of Jesus Christ understands what the grace of God is: not a compromise of His nature and character, but an act of love by which the guilty party (sinful man) is punished for his sins and is being made spotless and pure as the eternal bride of the Lamb of God. God in the flesh is the only one qualified to undertake the most amazing feat in history. As God, He was spotless and perfect. As a human, He lived as the guilty party, although He never sinned. He took on Himself the punishment of all men for the sins of humanity.

The combination of these deceptions – the nature of God and man, a false reconciliation leading to a false gospel, and a message of universal salvation – lead perfectly into the next great con being perpetrated on professing Christians.

The Church Growth Movement

Pastors are to be men of God, dedicated to His Word, and passionate and empowered to preach His Word to convict men of their sins, inspiring them to desire holy living. Today, more and more pastors act like secular CEOs, interested in growing numbers and finances and defining success as a large church. Christian seminaries are spitting out graduates who are trained to lead and inspire using secular techniques while coming out with little to no knowledge or wisdom regarding God's Word. Churches like Willow Creek, which long ago sold out to the secular Church Growth Movement, hold "Global Leadership Summits" that emphasize secular leadership principles over biblical leadership principles. They parade men like Bill Clinton, Rob Bell, Bono, and Senator Cory Booker in front of tens of thousands, touting them as models of leadership. And a growing number of phony Christians hang on every word because they want to be leaders.

Global Leadership Summits like these feed the growth of American Christianity at the sacrifice of Biblical Christianity. When churches and seminaries abandon the ways of God for the ways of men, many will be seduced into a false religion that can save no man. And since many Christians choose to remain biblically illiterate and trust whatever the pastor or televangelist says about the Bible, they will remain in a growing darkness that one day may cost them their eternal souls.

Word of Faith Theology

When we think that man at his core is good, we easily come to believe that somehow God owes us something. That if we do something good, God is forced to bless us right now. Word of Faith theology fits perfectly into American Christianity! Our nation's founders recognized that only submission to and reliance upon God could grow and sustain our nation. But somewhere along the line, as God blessed our nation with incredible prosperity and wealth, we started thinking *we* were the ones responsible for the prosperity. Americans are hardworking people of ingenuity. But failing to recognize that God alone is able to produce anything of lasting good has led to pride and arrogance. We start to believe that we are the cause of good things rather than the recipient of blessings from God. Somehow God owes us something because we are Americans who profess to be Christians!

That last line fits perfectly within Word of Faith theology: God is at our beck and call because of who we are. The Scriptures are twisted mercilessly to claim that Jesus' death on the cross insures us of health, wealth, and prosperity as long as we have enough faith. Our faith alone somehow mandates that God provide money and good health. God has no say in the matter and He is actually the one who is now serving us instead of the other way around.

This harmful heresy again springs from failing to understand the nature and character of God. And the twists and turns these false teachers use to justify their unbiblical teachings are incredible. Claims like "Well, we now know that Jesus actually had a rich woman as a benefactor who supplied all his needs," Paul's inability to remove the thorn in his flesh being a result of his lack of faith, and some of the claims that Jesus cannot directly intervene against demons unless we act, are undermining the nature of God and wrongly elevating the status of men.

For a more thorough look and documentation on Word of Faith

theology, please read my book *American Christianity's Adultery with Secular Culture.* Suffice it to say that as America has prospered, we have become greedy, always asking – no, *demanding* – more from God.

A False Equivalency: Confusing Spiritual and Political Issues

The social justice movement is permeating every denomination of American Christianity. It elevates the good works Jesus taught us to carry out over the gospel message itself. Rather than social justice being the *effects* of Biblical Christianity, it is elevated to the *cause* of Jesus coming to earth. Some of the leaders of the movement are also in error on several critical doctrines of the Christian faith that feed their passion for social justice.

Earlier I mentioned the stance our Christian radio station had to take to speak out against Jim Wallis of Sojourners being invited as a keynote speaker at an annual Christian music event. Early on we tried to reason with the festival organizers, privately sharing our concerns in the hopes it would not lead to a public falling-out. The president of the Christian organization asked if I would be willing to speak to Wallis, sure that if I did, I would see him as a mainline Evangelical. I agreed and had two direct conversations with Wallis.

In the final talk, Wallis stated a belief to me that exposed the fallacy of his belief system. He defended his social justice platform by stating that Jesus could not return to earth until mankind had eradicated all poverty, pollution, and social injustice. We make the world "pristine" in his words and *then* Jesus can return. When I confronted him with the prophetic Scriptures where Jesus said the world would be on the brink of destruction with rampant evil just before He returns, Wallis said, "Oh, so you're one of *them!*"

Wallis's faulty doctrines go right back to undermining the nature and character of God and elevating the status of man. The arrogance of thinking that sinful man, whose sin is the cause of all evil in this world, can make this world perfect again is Babylonian thinking. It gives man power and authority only God has, elevating us and diminishing Him.

This manifests itself in how many Christians fall for the deception of radical environmentalism. Environmental degeneration is the effect of sin. God will one day restore all things to perfection when He creates a new heaven and earth. Should we do all we can to be excellent stewards of this world that God has given us temporary dominion over? Absolutely. But to believe that we have the answer when our sin is the problem undermines God and elevates man. That's Babylonian thinking.

Other issues like immigration are political issues that progressives have falsely promoted as spiritual issues. Commands from Jesus to help the poor and visit the sick have been elevated over the Great Commission of sharing the gospel and making disciples. Every nation has the right to dictate and enforce immigration laws they see as best for their nation. To paint people who support limited and legal immigration policies as if we are disobeying Jesus, however, is spiritual malpractice and clever deception.

On the other side of the equation is how spiritual issues are being presented as political. Abortion, homosexual marriage, and gender fluidity and confusion are subjects Christians are being bullied into silence about because there is no place in the church for them. God is perfectly clear on these issues in His Word. Life begins when God decides it, sex is confined to being between a married man and woman, and gender is established by God as either male or female. But because we do not spend serious time in God's Word, we are easy pickings for false teachers and politicians who masquerade as Christians, spies sent into the camp to create confusion and infighting.

Discounting the Old Testament

Pastor Andy Stanley is famous for teaching that Christians should unhitch from the Old Testament teachings because, in his words, "Jesus and the Apostles taught that to the early church." But nowhere in God's Word are we told to ignore or dismiss the Old Testament teachings and narrative. So why would Stanley and others preach this? One can only speculate, but I believe it is a continuation of the false argument that somehow Jesus "changed" the God of the Old Testament. That somehow God is no longer a just, righteous, and holy God who will send Jesus back one day to judge all men. This undermines the nature of God, proposing that God's nature is fluid and subject to change. As if God somehow saw the error of His ways and changed His nature to one of only love, mercy, and no longer requiring a sacrifice for sin. But this would make the cross a lie, and therein lies the danger, because there is no way sinful man can be reconciled to God except through the atoning sacrifice of the cross!

Other emergent teachers have said that if God had Jesus killed on the cross, that is tantamount to "cosmic child abuse." To undermine the necessity of the substitutionary atonement of Jesus Christ on the cross is to diminish God and elevate sinful man, a common thread in American Christianity. It subtly proposes that somehow God meets us halfway: we change a little and He changes a little. This is pure blasphemy, yet it is being consciously or unconsciously taught in a growing number of churches.

Being reconciled to God is not a matter of man and God compromising somewhere in the middle. Reconciliation is man surrendering to God; it is acknowledging that He is perfect and we are sinners and that He is right and we are wrong.

Teaching and Promoting Human Unity over Biblical Unity

In John 17 Jesus prays that His disciples would be *one* like He and the Father are *one*. We start by seeing how Jesus and the Father are one in John 14.

> *Philip said to him, "Lord, show us the Father, and it is*
> *enough for us." Jesus said to him, "Have I been with you so*
> *long, and you still do not know me, Philip? Whoever has*
> *seen me has seen the Father. How can you say, 'Show us the*
> *Father'? Do you not believe that I am in the Father and the*
> *Father is in me? The words that I say to you I do not speak*
> *on my own authority, but the Father who dwells in me does*
> *his works. Believe me that I am in the Father and the Father*
> *is in me, or else believe on account of the works themselves."*
> (John 14:8-11)

Jesus stated that every word He spoke and every action He took was directly from the Father working in and through Him. This is what it means to be "one with God." In John 17 Jesus lists several characteristics of His followers being one with God:

- They receive the Word and believe it completely (verse 8).

- The world hates them because they do not behave as the world does (verse 14).

- They are not of this world, meaning they are not seduced by the trappings of this world and its beliefs and values (verse 16).

- They are being sanctified in truth, meaning they rightly handle the Word of God and the teachings of Jesus (verse 17).

When believers exhibit these fruits they become one with God, meaning they are in complete agreement with God and their words and actions bear witness to that. The true believer is being completely reconciled to God in belief, thought, and action. We are becoming more like Jesus in character, word, and deed with each passing day. So the characteristics of true Christian unity Jesus gave us are:

- Complete belief and trust in the Word of God

- Being hated by the world

- Not seduced by the beliefs and actions of this fallen world

- Sanctified in truth by rightly handling the Word of God

But the false human unity being taught in American Christianity is the opposite of true biblical unity. It teaches that we should set aside any conflict or differences in our beliefs, regardless of what the Bible teaches, and become one. The prevailing message is that when *we* are one, than we will be one with God, regardless of serious doctrinal differences. What do we see in American Christianity?

- A lack of trust in God's Word with it being called into question as antiquated or just the writings of men

- Embracing the world and seeking to be loved by it

- Allowing the beliefs and values of this sinful world to infiltrate the church

- Questioning the Word of God as truth using human reasoning and enlightenment

The unity being taught in American Christianity is the exact opposite of what Jesus wants of His disciples. Continuing the pattern, it elevates the status of man while diminishing the status of God.

Summary

A summary of doctrinal differences between Biblical and American Christianity:

TOPIC	*BIBLICAL CHRISTIANITY*	*AMERICAN CHRISTIANITY*
Nature of God	Righteous, just, never changing	Only love, evolves to meet man halfway
Nature of Man	Completely sinful and rebellious	Generally good
Man's Salvation	Only through the substitutionary atonement of Jesus	Varying and evolving as God adapts to us
The Old Testament	Important spiritually and historically, establishing God's unchanging nature	Acknowledged but not taught, as it might confuse people; perhaps antiquated, no longer applicable
Reconciliation with God	Sinful man is reconciled to God through the gospel as man surrenders to God	God changes and/or compromises to be reconciled with the beliefs of man
Gospel of Salvation	Acknowledge our sins and rebellion; repent; have complete faith and trust in Jesus alone to be saved; commit to obey God and be sanctified	"Invite Jesus into your heart" with no responsibility for heartfelt confession, repentance, or change of behavior
Church Growth	Individual members growing in holiness and sanctification	Increase numbers of attendance and finances

Church Unity	Believers becoming "one" with God as Jesus was leads to true spiritual unity based on the Bible's teachings	Professing believers setting aside important doctrinal differences in the name of tolerance or love
Christians "Judging"	The fruits of professing believers to teach, correct, and, when necessary, rebuke others for their benefit	Don't ever judge
Abortion, Sex, and Gender	Clear spiritual issues with clear biblical answers	"Political" issues to be discounted or ignored

With each passing year, American Christianity strays further from Biblical Christianity. But it has happened at such a gradual pace that most professing Christians are not aware of what has happened. If you stare at the hour hand of a clock for sixty minutes you will probably never notice its movement. Then you take a step back and realized it has indeed moved. But when you watch the minute or seconds hand you see the march of time. There is one other important factor to consider when assessing the direction of your church: Who is influencing whom?

Biblical Christianity: Disciples of Jesus Christ are spiritually mature to the point we are able to influence culture, leading more lost people to the truth of God and the gospel of salvation. We increasingly become light and salt to a dying world as Jesus' ambassadors. The church affects the secular culture. We speak the truth in love on important spiritual issues like abortion, homosexuality, and gender in order to be God's ambassadors of hope to a lost world.

American Christianity: Rather than affecting secular culture, the church is influenced *by* secular culture. The ways of the world are adopted in order to be more seeker friendly so the church can grow superficially through bigger numbers in attendance. It continually seeks compromise with the world it loves, thinking it is expanding God's kingdom. Instead, it is doing what Jesus accused the Pharisees of doing: thinking they are making converts but actually leading them to become *child*[ren] *of hell* (Matthew 23:15). Spiritual issues are identified as "political" and are to be ignored by the church so as not to cause dissension and to be seen instead as loving to the world.

Life and institutions are dynamic rather than static. Nothing stays the same forever except God. Individuals and churches either grow closer to God or drift further away from Him. Church doctrines either grow closer to God's perfect Word or drift into worldly humanism.

Maybe the church or denomination you have been in for years has historically been rock solid on Christian theology and is starting to slowly drift away from God's truth. Like watching the hour hand on a clock, the movement is so subtle you cannot see it. Suddenly, things have changed dramatically and you might find yourself in a church or denomination that was once solid and is now becoming more like American Christianity. How can we spot early warning signs of a spiritual drift? When is it time to either leave a church or stay there in hopes of influencing leadership to abandon the slippery slope they are standing upon? Next, we will take a look at how we have drifted from Biblical Christianity to American Christianity and the serious consequences of this spiritual drift, along with how you can spot troubling trends in the church that might indicate a slide into American Christianity.

Chapter Two

Early Warning Signs of American Christianity Infecting Your Church

---

The vast majority of churches slipping into American Christianity these days did not start out intending to do so. No doubt they were established by men seeking to glorify God by reaching the lost and equipping the saints for the work of the Holy Spirit in the church. But the following dangerous series of incidents have led many churches to compromise and even accept secular culture within the church:

- Public institutions (government, education, and media) were infected with secular humanists and liberals who proposed human solutions to spiritual problems. God's Word was increasingly ignored and mocked as antiquated. Human reasoning was elevated, replacing these antiquated biblical solutions to world and personal problems.

- As a result, the number of people who abandoned church was growing. The American church was finding that the traditional method of reaching the lost with the gospel (contrasting God's holiness and standards with man's sinful, rebellious nature) was no longer working. New methods would be required and the church reasoned it had to figure out how to meet people's needs in order to attract them to church.

- As a result, *reconciliation* had to be redefined to enhance church growth. Instead of reconciliation to God defined as sinful man surrendering to a just, righteous, and holy God who never changes, it was subtly presented as God meeting us halfway. Jesus just wants to be *in* your heart instead of giving you a new heart. God just wants you to love Him, not obey and worship Him. This American Christianity revised definition of reconciliation with God feeds our flesh perfectly but does nothing to transform our decrepit spiritual condition. We are still in rebellion against God and demanding that He reconcile to our flesh instead of us surrendering to Him.

- Peter Drucker influenced pastors like Robert Schuller, Rick Warren, and Bill Hybels, convincing them that by adopting worldly business principles the church could grow. As pastors started behaving more like corporate CEOs instead of shepherds of Christ's flock, growth in numbers trumped the spiritual growth of individual church members. People were flocking to churches to hear what Jesus could do for them in the realm of happiness and wealth instead of hearing a call to surrender to God and grow in holiness.

- As megachurches started popping up all over the nation, suddenly pastors saw a great influx of attendance and financial support. Having tasted the "fruit," they wanted more. Suddenly, money became the most important thing in many of these churches. Money was justified as necessary for reaching lost people and churches started embarking more on church programs, hoping to keep the "customers" happy. Subtly but effectively, the church replaced God's Word as the answer to all man's questions and problems.

- Suddenly flush with earthly success, many pastors started feeling an "anointing from God." Pride replaced humility and now it was necessary to insulate these megachurch pastors from questioning or criticism. Elder boards became more entrenched with business professionals and "yes-men" loyal to a man instead of to God.

- As professing believers became more enamored with the messenger (an eloquent pastor) than the message (the complete Word of God), these pastors were elevated to a stature reserved for God alone: One who should never be questioned. The small-group method was established. It was proposed as a way to get people into God's Word, but in reality it has too often become a means of controlling the flock rather than protecting and growing it. The group would receive instructions from church leadership on what to study and how to apply it. Church members were becoming dependent on the teachings of men instead of the Word of God.

- While all this was unfolding, greed took hold of the hearts of many professing Christians, fueled by false teachings like the Word of Faith movement. Suddenly, God was a ticket to economic prosperity. Suddenly, the church became more about meeting the temporal needs of its members than the state of their eternal souls. More and more time at the pulpit was dedicated to addressing finances and other temporal issues instead of preaching the holiness and wrath of God against sin and unrepentant sinners.

- False doctrines like Word of Faith and others are easily refuted by the Bible . . . which leads to the final dangerous step into American Christianity: In order to control and manipulate members, they must remain ignorant of God's Word. The pastor or assigned small group leader must make certain that the flock remains ignorant and dependent on what the church teaches. Teach the exact verses and interpretation laid out by church leadership without deviation. And if certain members begin to question those teachings, label them as troublemakers or dividers. Discredit them by any means so the system is not questioned.

This brings us full circle back to the beginning of this timeline. American Christianity, facing pressure and opposition from a growing secular society, decided compromise rather than biblical truth was the answer to growth. And once you make that decision, there is no going back. The prosperity and wealth many churches are experiencing cannot be sustained without continuing to pander to secular society and the customers who come to the church to be pampered rather than challenged, who come to find comfort rather than spiritual growth, and who come to be told how wonderful they are instead of how their continuing sin brings shame and dishonor to the name of the Lord.

The enemy has been so successful in getting American Christianity to wander from the Bible that churches will be easy pickings for the radical activism of the far left we are seeing unfold right before our eyes. Churches and ministries are being sued, Bibles are being called "hate speech," and economic pressure is coming from federal, state, and local governments through new laws and requirements. Pressure is being applied by the LGBTQ movement to not only accept but also approve of their lifestyles. Churches are beginning to accept homosexuality and gender confusion as normal and even biblical. American Christianity has made itself extremely vulnerable by abandoning the Word of God for the beliefs of man. As the attacks ramp up, churches will be forced into further complicity with the world or be shut down. They will submit to the world and justify it by saying their existence as a church is necessary and is actually pleasing to God, when in reality they slouch more and more toward Babylon.

This shift from Biblical Christianity to American Christianity does not happen overnight. It starts out slowly with a single compromise or two, and left unchecked, it grows into pride and potential apostasy. If caught early enough and confronted, a church can be salvaged. But if left unquestioned, it becomes a juggernaut headed down a dangerous path, leading many astray.

The chart at the end of chapter 1 contrasting Biblical Christianity with American Christianity can serve as a bellwether for observing the trends in your church. Are the teachings of your church lining up with the Bible or American Christianity on these important issues?

- The nature and character of God

- The nature of man

- The gospel of salvation

- Who is being reconciled to whom between God and men

- Church growth
- Abortion, sexuality, and gender
- The handling of the Old Testament
- Unity in the body and Christian judgment

I will give you some guidelines and things to watch out for in each of these dangerous pitfalls.

The Nature of God

Does your church teach a lot about sin? Or is it just occasionally touched upon? Are you reminded and challenged about ongoing sin in your life? What is taught as God's purpose for your life? Is it abundance? Or is it the necessity of the professing believer to be transformed more and more into the image of Jesus Christ (increased holiness)?

Is God's unchanging nature discussed? His eternal righteousness, justice, and holiness? His hatred of sin and unrepentant sinners and His coming wrath against them? The truth that Jesus will return one day to judge all men and that most will be damned to eternal separation from God? Is biblical prophecy taught in the church? Or is it ignored or purposefully disregarded?

The Nature of Man

Are you being reminded of what Paul taught, that grace is not a license to continue sinning? Or are you being taught that your sins no longer matter to God? Are you being reminded that you still have a sinful nature (Romans 7) even though you are a new creation? Are you being taught the need for godly sorrow when you continue to sin? Or are you being taught that confession and repentance is a one-time thing?

Are you being challenged about potential gods you continue to worship by your actions? Money, entertainment, sports, or even friends and family? Are you encouraged to be in a true small group of committed believers who can hold you accountable – those you can be open with and accept rebuke from because you know they love you? Or are you under the spiritual umbrella of a church so large that there can be no intimate sharing and accountability? Do you prefer to remain anonymous at a church so large that you can hide your sin? Or do you truly seek accountability to God and His Word?

The Gospel of Salvation (Reconciliation to God)

Does or *can* your church leaders accurately teach the full gospel of salvation and reconciliation to God? Are you taught that even one sin by you is so abhorrent to God that it warrants eternal damnation without His grace and forgiveness? Is the wrath of God ever taught in your church? What about God's righteous and just nature demanding payment for your sins?

Is the gospel message being taught one of "Jesus loves you so much He died for your sins" or "The just and gracious God of the universe looked down on hopelessly lost and sinful man, and sent His only begotten Son, Jesus Christ – God in the flesh – to die on a cross for the sin of repentant men and be raised from the dead to prove God's power over death for those who confess their sinful nature, repent of their wicked beliefs and actions, and completely trust in Jesus alone for their salvation, and to identify a people of His own who will love, honor, and obey Him, set apart as a people peculiar to this world"?

Does the "gospel" taught in your church even talk about reconciliation? A surrender of man to the ways of God? Or is your church subtly teaching that reconciliation with God means that both God and man compromise? That God has set aside His righteous and just nature that demands a severe payment for sin and now the only part of His nature is love?

Are you being taught and equipped with the complete gospel in order that you might share it with your family, friends, and fellow employees? Or are you being taught to "just love on them"? Does your church distinguish between the biblical and human definition of *love*? Are you being taught how to speak the truth in love to people who are lost and living a lifestyle that God will condemn? Or are you being taught to just accept them because "God doesn't make mistakes"?

Church Growth

Ask them to define a "successful" church. Ask them what the Bible teaches about the purpose and actions of the church.

Is the goal of your church leadership to grow in the number of members? Or to help individual committed disciples of Jesus Christ grow in the grace and knowledge of Him (2 Peter 3:18)?

Is the leadership structure of your church lining up with the Bible's teachings where a pastor is a shepherd and teacher? Or is he more of a CEO who manages every aspect of the church? Does the pastor submit to the elders or dictate policy to them? Are your elders comprised of men of spiritual maturity and experience or men of business and worldly experience?

Are the budget and expenditures of the church open and accountable to members? Or is it "none of your business" how funds are being spent? Is your pastor being adequately compensated to provide for his family or is he forced to struggle to make ends meet? Or, is he living a life of relative luxury compared to many in the church?

Are you being taught that tithing to your church is a biblical requirement of believers? Or are you being taught to be generous with all God has given you and to give as God's Spirit influences you to give?

How would your leadership answer this question: "Which would you prefer – a church with lots of members or a smaller church where people are growing in holiness?" (Do not let them cop out with an answer of a blending of both).

Does your church discourage believers gathering on their own for Bible studies without church leadership's knowledge or blessing? Or does every study have to be approved by church leadership?

If your church decides to do a capital campaign for a new, beautiful church building, how would they answer the question of why a simple, functional building is not sufficient? If their answer is that a beautiful building will attract new members, ask them what the Word of God says in Acts 2 about church growth. What spurred true church growth in the early church – men or God? If a new, beautiful building will attract new members, ask them what happens when the next church builds a newer, more beautiful building?

One way to determine if your church is immersed in the Church Growth Movement that sacrifices biblical truth for growth in numbers is by listening carefully to what is and is not preached from God's Word. What is *not* taught is just as important as what *is* taught.

Using the Bible As an Instrument of Deception

This is not a misprint. And it might go against everything you have come to understand about the Bible. But to deny the real possibility that the Word of God could be used to deceive you is to deny the Bible itself.

> *Then the devil took him to the holy city and set him on the pinnacle of the temple and said to him, "If you are the Son of God, throw yourself down, for it is written, 'He will command his angels concerning you,' and 'On their hands they will bear you up, lest you strike your foot against a stone.'"*
> *Jesus said to him, "Again it is written, 'You shall not put the Lord your God to the test.'"* (Matthew 4:5-7)

Satan, the father of lies, tried to use the very Word of God (out of context) to tempt Jesus Christ. Do we really think he would not use the same tactic against us? Indeed, through the faulty human institution of American Christianity, Satan has found a new ally to spread clever deception disguised as the Word of God. And make no mistake, he has been very successful in his clever deception. In American Christianity God's Word is read and taught apart from correct context, and that's all the enemy needs to sow seeds of doubt and confusion.

> *But I am afraid that as the serpent deceived Eve by his cunning, your thoughts will be led astray from a sincere and pure devotion to Christ. For if someone comes and proclaims another Jesus than the one we proclaimed, or if you receive a different spirit from the one you received, or if you accept a different gospel from the one you accepted, you put up with it readily enough.* (2 Corinthians 11:3-4)

> *And what I am doing I will continue to do, in order to undermine the claim of those who would like to claim that in their boasted mission they work on the same terms as we*

do. For such men are false apostles, deceitful workmen, disguising themselves as apostles of Christ. And no wonder, for even Satan disguises himself as an angel of light. So it is no surprise if his servants, also, disguise themselves as servants of righteousness. Their end will correspond to their deeds.
(2 Corinthians 11:12-15)

To help put this into clearer perspective, when was the last time, if ever, your pastor preached on these verses or warned at all about false teachers infiltrating the church? If he never has, one has to wonder why. Could it be that if church members are taught how to spot false teachers the church leadership might be open to scrutiny? These are the difficult questions we must ask if we are serious about rescuing people from American Christianity and returning them to the full truth of God's Word.

Biblical Christianity teaches the full message of the Bible in correct context. There is no agenda other than God being glorified and sinful men being reconciled to God through the gospel message. American Christianity teaches snippets from the Bible to support their human agenda and lures people into a false sense of security. Here are some of the more obvious examples of how American Christianity uses select verses to deceive people:

"For God so loved the world, that he gave his only Son, that whoever believes in him should not perish but have eternal life. For God did not send his Son into the world to condemn the world, but in order that the world might be saved through him." (John 3:16-17)

American Christianity uses these two verses to suggest the possibility of universal salvation, contrary to what the Bible teaches.

"Whoever believes in him is not condemned, but whoever does not believe is condemned already, because he has not believed in the name of the only Son of God. And this is the judgment: the light has come into the world, and people loved the darkness rather than the light because their works were evil." (John 3:18-19)

Biblical Christianity teaches all four of these verses in John 3 to refute universal salvation or the illusion that many more will go to heaven than the Bible actually states.

"Judge not, that you be not judged." (Matthew 7:1)

American Christianity teaches this single verse out of context to criticize or condemn any Christian who makes any judgment about anyone. Biblical Christianity teaches the complete context of what the Bible says about judging others:

- We are to judge the beliefs and behaviors of professing Christians to point out contradictions in order to help them.

- We are to judge the beliefs and fruit of false teachers so they may be exposed.

"If anyone hears my words and does not keep them, I do not judge him; for I did not come to judge the world but to save the world." (John 12:47)

American Christianity uses this single verse out of context to claim that Jesus doesn't ever judge, so we shouldn't either.

"If anyone hears my words and does not keep them, I do not judge him; for I did not come to judge the world but to save the world. The one who rejects me and does not receive my words has a judge; the word that I have spoken will judge him on the last day." (John 12:47-48)

Biblical Christianity teaches these verses in correct context to show that the first time Jesus came was to offer salvation, but He will return one day to judge all men with His Word.

"That they may all be one, just as you, Father, are in me, and I in you, that they also may be in us, so that the world may believe that you have sent me." (John 17:21)

American Christianity quotes this single verse to advance the idea that if we as Christians are united and are not allowing biblical doctrines to be divisive, then we will be one with God. This is used as an excuse to expand the church by discrediting biblical doctrines that might not be attractive to people.

> *"I have given them your word, and the world has hated them because they are not of the world, just as I am not of the world."* (John 17:14)

Biblical Christianity sees verse 14 as the *cause* for verse 21. Since the world will hate us like they hate the teachings of Jesus, we should be united around the truth of God's Word rather than compromising it to appease the world, in order to encourage one another as the hatred of this world grows more intense.

> *"Touch not my anointed ones, do my prophets no harm!"* (1 Chronicles 16:22)

American Christianity uses this verse to silence any Christian who questions the teachings of the Word of Faith movement or any church leader who might be leading the church members astray. Biblical Christianity understands that in this verse God is warning people to not harm a *true* prophet from God: one who speaks His Word accurately.

> *"Again I say to you, if two of you agree on earth about anything they ask, it will be done for them by my Father in heaven. For where two or three are gathered in my name, there am I among them."* (Matthew 18:19-20)

American Christianity presents these verses to promote Word of Faith theology or give Christians a false hope that if two or three want God to do something, He will. Biblical Christianity correctly teaches that Jesus was talking about the need for church discipline and confronting unrepentant sinners, something American Christianity fears for loss of numbers.

> *Anyone who does not love does not know God, because God is love.* (1 John 4:8)

American Christianity uses this single verse to dismiss the eternal nature of God (righteous, just, and holy) in order to promote compromise between man and God instead of the true gospel of reconciliation where sinful man surrenders to God's will. Biblical Christianity can accurately teach how God's righteous and just nature are not in conflict with His love and mercy.

There is also an overriding theme to how American Christianity promotes what the life of a Christian should look like. It touts the freedoms and benefits of salvation while dismissing the Bible's call for holy living and often ignores the numerous Scriptures that call on Christians to endure potential suffering and persecution for their beliefs. These verses undermine some of the tenets of American Christianity and do nothing to attract new church members who prefer comfort over spiritual growth. A sad effect of ignoring these clear teachings is that when church members go through periods of ridicule or suffering, they get frustrated because they have never been taught about the Bible's warnings and how to respond in a way that their joy will not suffer. This can lead to anger with God and in some cases even lead people to abandon the faith because God cannot be trusted when they are allowed to suffer.

Judging as Christians

Are you being taught that Christians are never allowed to judge others? Or are you being taught the correct role and purpose for Christians judging the fruits of other professing believers? Does your church have an official church discipline policy in place? Has it ever been used and why? Propose this scenario: You have an affair with another woman; your wife confronts you and you are unrepentant. She brings it to the elders who confront you; you remain unrepentant, justifying your adultery with human understanding. What would you as elders do?

Ask if your church would allow unrepentant homosexuals, transgenders, adulterers, or thieves to be members of the church. Should they even be allowed to attend? Indefinitely or on what conditions?

Ask them if Jesus ever did or ever will judge anyone. Then ask for their interpretation of these verses:

> "If anyone hears my words and does not keep them, I do not judge him; for I did not come to judge the world but to save the world. The one who rejects me and does not receive my words has a judge; the word that I have spoken will judge him on the last day." (John 12:47-48)

Ask what Jesus meant by *the word that I have spoken will judge him on the last day.* Is Jesus talking about a single verse or two or the entire Word of God?

Ask if Christians are supposed to judge unbelievers. What does it mean to love the sinner? Does it mean we approve of or excuse them living in a way contradictory to what the Bible teaches? If not, how do we confront them in their sin with truth and grace?

Church Unity

Ask your leaders exactly what church unity looks like. Ask them for a specific definition, not just vague statements. Is a church in unity if some members disagree with clear biblical instruction and doctrine, as long as other members are okay with it?

Ask which is more important: truth or unity. If you can only have one, which should we choose?

Which biblical doctrines are necessary for uniformity for church members? Which doctrines allow for respectful disagreement and discussion? Is there even a place for biblical doctrine in the church? Or is each member on his own to believe what he will believe? Ask if the breaking of fellowship is ever warranted. And if so, what would be some causes? Ask for a biblical explanation of Matthew 18:15-17. What did Jesus mean when He said, *"let him be to you as a Gentile and a tax collector"*?

Spiritual or Political Issues?

The past few years have seen a radical change in American culture. As few as ten years ago the vast majority of Americans, and certainly professing Christians, believed homosexuality was a sin. But since the Supreme Court ruling legalizing homosexual marriage, a strong majority of Americans, including many Christians, believe it is acceptable in God's eyes.

Up until a couple years ago no one would question if gender could be fluid. You were born male or female and that could not change. As I write this book, gender dysphoria, a fictitious condition trumped by secularists and the medical community, has become epidemic in our society. Children as young as nine years old are undergoing irreversible hormone treatments and even permanent surgeries to attempt to change their gender, something that is quite impossible.

Secular society has convinced us these are political and human issues instead of spiritual issues. Every time a Christian speaks out against the acceptance of homosexuality or gender fluidity he is labeled a homophobe and a bigot. The church is being bullied into silence on these core issues of sin, and because we want to be seen as loving and accepting, and perhaps deep down are worried about our non-profit tax advantages, we sit silently by and dismiss these issues as political with no place for them in the church's teachings or discussions. The result? Our children are thrown into confusion as more and more of their friends express confusion about their gender and the church has no answers. Since the church cannot address this dilemma, our youth assume what their friends are experiencing is real and justifiable, and it begins to affect the thought processes and beliefs of children in our churches. And we wonder why up to 80 percent of professing Christian youth leave the faith in high school or college.

Abortion kills more than one million innocent children every year in our nation. When is the last time your church discussed this genocide? Can your church leaders point out where God says life begins in the Bible? Or are they cowering behind science and political issues? One of Babylon's greatest sins was child sacrifice. Isn't abortion exactly that? But instead of sacrificing our children to a false god, we do something worse. We approve of abortion to justify our sexual desires and our financial greed of not being burdened by having to raise a child. We worship ourselves at the cost of allowing innocent children to be sacrificed for our greed and convenience!

I worked for a strong pro-life organization before I came to Q90 FM. We saw studies that showed that more than 80 percent of women suffer physical, emotional, and spiritual pain from having an abortion. God's mercy and grace can alleviate that pain by them being reconciled to Him. But since we cower as a church from addressing this genocide, we allow thousands of professing Christian women to bear the emotional and spiritual scars for the rest of their lives because we will not address the single greatest issue of genocide in the history of the world. Hitler had six million Jews murdered. America has now murdered more than fifty million babies since abortion was legalized. Face the facts: We are worse than Hitler on this subject. But American Christianity turns a blind eye.

The Handling of the Old Testament

Does your church even teach from the Old Testament, other than the Psalms and perhaps Proverbs? It is the Word of God, so if they do not or just barely ever touch on it we must ask why. Perhaps they are ashamed of God who in the Old Testament had His people wipe out entire cities of evil people. Perhaps they cannot wrap their heads around why God would destroy all human life except for Noah and his family in a world-wide flood. Or, as an increasing number of self-professed Christians believe, perhaps your leadership thinks these are just fictitious stories.

I believe none of these are the overriding answer. I believe the real answer, based on hundreds of discussions I have had with pastors, is this: They cannot reconcile the Old and New Testaments when it comes to understanding God's nature and character. They cannot reconcile God's wrath with God's love and grace. They cannot explain a simple question like a listener once asked me: "If Jesus did not come to abolish the law, why are we no longer bound to obey it to be saved?" Or another asked, "If the law no longer applies to us as Christians, why is homosexuality still considered a sin, yet we do not stone adulterers and are now allowed to eat pork and shrimp?" Or still another: "If Allah of the Qur'an is a false god because he orders the murder of anyone who opposes Islam, how do we explain God ordering His people to kill all the inhabitants of some cities in the Old Testament?" Serious students of the Bible can correctly answer these sincere questions, but I have met only a handful of pastors who can. What does this say about the condition of many churches?

If your church leaders cannot correctly explain how to reconcile the Old and New Testaments, particularly concerning God's unchanging nature, the law and grace, and how we are to deal with sexual sins, you are in a church headed into American Christianity where doctrine is ignored or explained away, and personal feelings and subjective morality is king. If your church leaders cannot prove that Islam, the world's fastest growing religion, is a religion of Antichrist, what makes us think they will not succumb to the coming one-world religion the Bible warns us about?

Which Way Is Your Church Trending?

The best of churches can err in the interpretation of biblical doctrines. And while certain doctrines like the nature of God and the gospel of salvation and reconciliation are not open to debate, there are many teachings in the Bible that are not as clear to us as we would like. For example, on issues of certain behaviors like the foods we eat or the drinking of alcohol, Paul speaks of being led by our conscience, presuming the Holy Spirit and not our sinful flesh is influencing our conscience.

So even though your church might be falling short of Biblical Christianity in one of the bellwethers listed above, it is more important that we identify the direction of the church than its current position (dynamic versus static). The church might be open to, or in the process of, correcting faulty man-made doctrines and returning to the Bible as its sole authority. We should show patience and be active in helping any way we can.

But if the opposite is true, and the church's direction is away from Biblical Christianity toward American Christianity, at some point you might have to choose if you should stay and hope to influence them positively, or pick up your pearls and find another church. How can we determine which direction a church in error is headed? By discerning the motives and the hearts of the men who are leading the church.

Pride or Humility

God and His Word are perfect. Every man, no matter how committed to Jesus, is some combination of right and wrong. It is vital that we establish a system to determine the intent of the church when in error, whether it be unintentional error or intentional deception. The way to determine this is to see how people react when they are confronted in their errors.

Recently we covered a story of a Christian church, led by T. D. Jakes, allowing Hindu Yoga into the church for a women's class. This is happening with increased regularity as churches seek to bring human thinking into the church to attract more members. I laid out on-air how a member of this church could address this concern with church leadership.

Yoga is clearly a direct form of Hindu worship, and the leaders of Yoga make little effort to hide this fact. In spite of the direct testimony of Yoga leaders themselves, some Christians justify Yoga as "belonging to no specific religion, just like prayer." This was one of the defenses put up in Jakes's church. So we come equipped to the meeting with church leadership with the very words of Yoga teachers to share when we are ready.

But a full frontal assault on leadership is not warranted or biblical. Church leadership is not above error or deception, so they must be given the chance to correct any serious error. Here is how I recommended a meeting go:

> Concerned member: "Would we ever allow unbiblical teachings or the worship of false gods into our church or any of its programs?"

> Church leader: "No, we would not." (If their answer is anything but this, you know all you need to know. Run from that church.)

> Concerned member: "I am glad to hear that. What would you do if you discovered a false teaching or idol worship had somehow infiltrated our church?"

> Church leader: "We would confront it and remove it immediately." (Again, if you receive any other answer, that is a strong warning sign.)

> Concerned member: "Our church is hosting Yoga classes. Here is the testimony of those teaching and marketing Yoga . . . it clearly identifies Yoga as a specifically Hindu method of worship and practice . . . ."

Then just sit silently and see how they respond. Do not let them off the hook by talking further; the pressure is now on them. The humble leader will be glad the error was pointed out and will immediately move to correct it. The prideful leader will start to make excuses or even pull rank in the hopes of proving himself spiritually superior to you. You have now biblically and respectfully confronted error in the church; the next move of church leadership will give you an indication of the direction they are headed.

Notice we did not start out by accusing the church leaders of heresy. There was a serious issue that was confronted with grace and truth, giving the leaders the initial benefit of the doubt. You were willing to consider that the error was one of ignorance, not of intent. Their own response exposed their motive and heart.

Jesus often asked questions of the Pharisees to expose the true intent of their hearts. Only after they publicly sided against Him did He start calling them *sons of the evil one* and *whitewashed tombs*. He first used questions to help them sort through their confused thought process and contradictions. As long as this is done in the spirit of how Jesus did it (with complete grace and truth), we can stand before God with a clear conscience, knowing our goal was to help the church, not harm it.

It is vital that we recognize the important difference between deceivers and those being deceived. Any one of us can be deceived about something, and church leadership is no exception. Something is introduced to us in a way that sounds appealing and truthful, and unless we are well grounded in the Bible and aware of the tactics used to deceive us, we can succumb to clever arguments: We are being deceived.

A deceiver is someone who consciously chooses to use deception and lies to fool others. He knows what he is stating is in error but sticks with it in the hopes of deceiving others for his gain. How can we tell the difference and react appropriately?

The first thing necessary to confronting deception, whether intentional or not, is to be able to spot it. This requires a solid understanding of the Word of God and a strong thought process that can see through half-truths presented. In a later chapter we will discuss ways we can guard our mind and heart against the deceptions infiltrating the church and how we can correctly interpret the Word of God as He intended it to be understood.

> *Indeed, all who desire to live a godly life in Christ Jesus will be persecuted, while **evil people and impostors will go on from bad to worse, deceiving and being deceived.** But as for you, continue in what you have learned and have firmly believed, knowing from whom you learned it and how from childhood you have been acquainted with the sacred writings, which are able to make you wise for salvation through faith in Christ Jesus. All Scripture is breathed out by God and profitable for teaching, for reproof, for correction, and for training in righteousness, that the man of God may be complete, equipped for every good work.* (2 Timothy 3:12-17, emphasis added)

Notice Paul says that deceivers and even those being deceived go from bad to worse, showing a cycle of degeneration within their thought processes and beliefs. We are witnessing this in American Christianity as a whole. Just the smallest of false teachings left uncorrected can swell into a church that is abandoning God's doctrines for those of men. Paul then gives us the solution: the Word of God given to man as an anchor of eternal truth. As we will discuss later, an inability to correctly interpret God's Word as He intended leads to first being deceived, and then if left uncorrected, it leads to becoming a deceiver as we double down on our own opinions and man-made doctrines out of pride. Without the correctly interpreted and applied Word of God, opinions can be presented and accepted as truth, while in reality they are the opposite of truth.

What Is Being Preached and How Is It Being Applied?

The early church was centered on the teachings of the apostles. New believers gathered to hear about the Old Testament Scriptures that pointed to Jesus Christ and the gospel and how to live their lives as believers in a world that was out to destroy them. The Scriptures were front and center.

I have noticed a dramatic shift in the way many sermons are delivered these days. Rather than the Word of God being the focal point of today's sermons, it often makes merely a token appearance at the beginning, with the bulk of the message centered on quaint little "life stories." Instead of preaching on the nature and character of God, and the requirement that the believer be transformed into the image of Jesus Christ, today's messages often take only a verse or two and then proceed to teach about how they can be applied to better our lives. This speaks to something we have been discussing: reconciliation.

The gospel of reconciliation is sinful man being reconciled to a holy God, and the fruit of this is man turning away from the sin that has ensnared him and living an increasingly holy life that glorifies God. It is surrendering to a righteous, just, and holy God, and seeking to be transformed into the image of Jesus Christ. "Reverse reconciliation" is the attempt to use the Scriptures in a way that promotes compromise between God and man. Instead of the Word of God convicting us of our sin and leading to spiritual brokenness, reverse reconciliation subtly introduces the idea that God is okay with our continuing sinful lives, and that His grace saved us and requires no ongoing sanctification in our lives. We can live our lives to the fullest, confident that our sins have been forgiven and free to pursue the life this world presents.

> For the grace of God has appeared, bringing salvation for
> all people, training us to renounce ungodliness and worldly
> passions, and to live self-controlled, upright, and godly lives
> in the present age, waiting for our blessed hope, the appear-
> ing of the glory of our great God and Savior Jesus Christ,
> who gave himself for us to redeem us from all lawlessness
> and to purify for himself a people for his own possession
> who are zealous for good works. Declare these things; exhort
> and rebuke with all authority. Let no one disregard you.
> (Titus 2:11-15)

I shared in my last book, *The Death of Christian Thought*, that a funda-mental problem in American Christianity is redefining the biblical word *grace*. Paul tells us in these verses that the same grace of God that saves us also begins to sanctify and perfect us into a people of God zealous to do His work. True salvation necessarily leads to a life of increased holiness. American Christianity, without blatantly exposing it, teaches that grace is a license to continue sinning.

Biblical Christianity delivers a consistent message that, while we are saved by God's grace, that same grace calls us to abandon the love of this world and be transformed into the image of Jesus Christ.

American Christianity uses God's grace as a license to continue loving things of this world while having just enough grace to be saved. It compromises God's call to holiness and perfection, teaching that because of His grace we can have "our best life now" instead of embracing sacrifice and maybe even suffering for the name of Jesus.

Look for this subtle difference in the message being preached. Are you being called to increased holiness and perfection by God's grace and Spirit? Or are you being taught how to be happy in this life?

Are the Church's Men Equipped and Spiritually Leading?

Are the Church's Women "Proverbs 31" Wives?

There is no gentle way to say this: Radical feminism is transforming our society and infiltrating American Christianity. And if you want the world to come down on you like a ton of bricks, just make that statement in public. Having said that, I believe the reason radical feminism has taken hold is because we as Christian men and husbands abused the authority God gave us over our wives. We became bosses rather than leaders to our wives.

A boss is someone who manipulates others for his benefit. A leader is someone who leads and serves for the benefit of others. As husbands we must understand that our wives are a precious gift from God, a gift that comes with serious responsibilities. Let's take a deep look at what a husband is according to God's Word.

> *I am the true vine, and my Father is the husbandman. Every branch in me that beareth not fruit he taketh away: and every branch that beareth fruit, he purgeth it, that it may bring forth more fruit.* (John 15:1-2 KJV)

How could God the Father be the *husbandman* to Jesus? Simple, when we take the time to use God's definitions for the words He gave us. The word *husbandman* means "land worker; tiller of the soil; a vine dresser." Remember when Jesus said this:

> *So Jesus said to them, "Truly, truly, I say to you, the Son can do nothing of his own accord, but only what he sees the Father doing. For whatever the Father does, that the Son does likewise."* (John 5:19)

> *"For I have not spoken on my own authority, but the Father who sent me has himself given me a commandment—what to say and what to speak. And I know that his commandment is eternal life. What I say, therefore, I say as the Father has told me."* (John 12:49-50)

Is Jesus a "husband"? *Husbands, love your wives, as Christ loved the church and gave himself up for her, that he might sanctify her, having cleansed her by the washing of water with the word, so that he might present the church to himself in splendor, without spot or wrinkle or any such thing, that she might be holy and without blemish. In the same way husbands should love their wives as their own bodies. He who loves his wife loves himself. For no one ever hated his own flesh, but nourishes and cherishes it, just as Christ does the church, because we are members of his body. "Therefore a man shall leave his father and mother and hold fast to his wife, and the two shall become one flesh." This mystery is profound, and I am saying that it refers to Christ and the church. However, let each one of you love his wife as himself, and let the wife see that she respects her husband."* (Ephesians 5:25-33)

> *Then I heard what seemed to be the voice of a great multitude, like the roar of many waters and like the sound of mighty peals of thunder, crying out, "Hallelujah! For the Lord our God the Almighty reigns.*

> *Let us rejoice and exult and give him the glory, for the marriage of the Lamb has come, and his Bride has made herself*

ready; it was granted her to clothe herself with fine linen, bright and pure"—for the fine linen is the righteous deeds of the saints. (Revelation 19:6-8)

Jesus is the perfect husband. He sacrificed for His bride (the true church of believers), giving His very life for her. He invested in her with His Word to create her as a spotless, pure bride to live with Him for eternity. We as the bride of Christ will be one with Him for eternity, cleaved to Him forever, serving, honoring, and loving Him.

The responsibility of a Christian husband is to help his wife bear amazing fruit for God by leading and serving her as Christ did for His bride, the true church. As God's steward of her, the husband enjoys amazing fruits from the relationship: peace, joy, honor, and emotional and physical intimacy.

The Bible is clear on the role of a wife: She is to honor and obey her husband. The only caveat to that is if her husband asks her to do something that would be a sin against God. That message will get you tar and feathered in this world and even in many professing churches these days, as radical feminism has taken over many of them. Women pastors, women as elders – all contradictory to the teachings of the Bible.

Let me be very clear: nowhere in Scripture do we see that God created woman as less than man or that He values women less than men. But a husband has God-given authority over his wife and the responsibility to help her produce amazing, eternal fruit for God. Women serve the church in amazing ways.

> *But as for you, teach what accords with sound doctrine. Older men are to be sober-minded, dignified, self-controlled, sound in faith, in love, and in steadfastness. Older women likewise are to be reverent in behavior, not slanderers or slaves to much wine. They are to teach what is good, and so train the young women to love their husbands and children, to be self-controlled, pure, working at home, kind, and submissive to their own husbands, that the word of God may not be reviled.* (Titus 2:1-5)

I do some counseling for Christian marriages from time to time. And inevitably all the problems Christian couples face are centered on a lack of understanding on what the Bible teaches about the roles and responsibilities of husbands and wives. Too many men act like bosses instead of biblical leaders. Too many women want to be the leader of the family instead of honoring and serving their husbands. When a marriage is centered on human understanding instead of godly wisdom, there is little to no hope. When I share these teachings with couples struggling, more often than not they decide the teachings are too harsh or antiquated – exactly what American Christianity is teaching about God's never-changing Word.

Undermining a Husband's Authority with His Wife

If you do a couple Internet searches on the following two topics, you will be alarmed at what you find: "women attracted to their pastors" and "patients attracted to their counselors."

You will see numerous studies, stories, and warnings of how women in particular develop amorous feelings for someone teaching or counseling them. Could this be why Paul, inspired by the Holy Spirit, taught this:

> For God is not a God of confusion but of peace. As in all
> the churches of the saints, the women should keep silent
> in the churches. For they are not permitted to speak, but
> should be in submission, as the Law also says. If there is
> anything they desire to learn, let them **ask their husbands**
> **at home**. For it is shameful for a woman to speak in church.
> (1 Corinthians 14:33-35, emphasis added)

No doubt these are very difficult verses, but they are breathed out through Paul by the Holy Spirit. To deny their truth or continuing wisdom is foolish and dangerous. Has your church ever shared or discussed these verses? Probably not, out of fear of repercussions.

When a pastor is elevated to a position above a husband, whether done consciously or not, the husband's leadership and responsibility to his wife are undermined, and this is exactly what Satan and his minions in secular society want! And sadly, by our silence in the church about the correct roles and responsibilities of husband and wife, we are reinforcing the destructive message of radical feminism.

Likewise, wives, be subject to your own husbands, so that even if some do not obey the word, they may be won without a word by the conduct of their wives, when they see your respectful and pure conduct. Do not let your adorning be external—the braiding of hair and the putting on of gold jewelry, or the clothing you wear— but let your adorning be the hidden person of the heart with the imperishable beauty of a gentle and quiet spirit, which in God's sight is very precious. For this is how the holy women who hoped in God used to adorn themselves, by submitting to their own husbands, as Sarah obeyed Abraham, calling him lord. And you are her children, if you do good and do not fear anything that is frightening. (1 Peter 3:1-6)

There is one more important reason that our churches need to start teaching the Bible's message on the role of husbands and wives: It is unfair to the pastor to ignore this any longer! It seems every month we hear another story of a pastor falling into sexual sin. Research shows many pastors struggling with Internet pornography. Our pastors are men, subject to temptation; and every time one of them falls, the world rejoices because it fuels the fire for their calls of "hypocrisy!" When women in the church find themselves attracted to the pastor as he teaches them the Word of God, we are placing our pastors in a very dangerous situation. This is why Paul admonished women to not interrupt the church with questions but to ask their husbands when they are at home. It reinforces the biblical role of the husband as teacher and provider for his wife.

What would your church leaders say if you brought them this information and asked if they would teach what God's Word says about it? Their response will give you a benchmark for the direction the church may be heading. If they reject it out of hand, your church is probably straying deeper into American Christianity and further from Biblical Christianity.

God established a certain order for us in His Word. When we see that order as antiquated, we stray into very dangerous waters. The failure of the professing church to teach the full counsel of God's Word is leading people into confusion and deception.

Does Your Church Truly Understand "The Story"?

In my last book I shared an example of reading a well-written murder novel. You read through hundreds of pages looking for clues as to "whodunit." The author takes you through unique stories and twists, and then finally, at the end of the novel you realize "The butler did it!" Now knowing that, go back and read the novel again. You will now see subtle clues left by the author that pointed to the butler all along. Having the foreknowledge of the guilty party gives you a deeper understanding and perspective on the book.

Let's face it. The Bible can be confusing at times even to the most avid reader and student. As finite and limited humans we struggle to understand an eternally holy and perfect God. *For now we see in a mirror dimly, but then face to face. Now I know in part; then I shall know fully, even as I have been fully known* (1 Corinthians 13:12). But using the example of the murder novel we can better understand the story of God and mankind when we know the end of that story.

How many times do we as Christians fail in our attempts to effectively share the gospel with our family and friends? We cower because we fear they may ask a question we cannot adequately answer, or we don't even attempt to share out of fear or shame. But what if you could give a comprehensive answer to any question a person might ask in less than two minutes? An answer that points them to the cause of every problem in this world and the eternal solution to those problems. Nice, huh? It goes beyond "nice"; it should be a requirement for anyone who claims to be a born-again believer, saved by God's grace. It's called biblical apologetics. Here is the wording I use to explain the big picture of the Bible in two minutes:

> God created all things and sustains all things. He has
> always existed and will always exist. He is perfect and thus
> never changes. God created all we see and He created man
> in His image to take dominion over all things. But man,
> given a free will to obey or disobey, chose disobedience and

rebellion against God. We decided we knew better than Him how things should be run. Man sinned against a holy and perfect God who had given him everything and had put only one restriction on him.

Sin entered the world and because of it, decay, destruction, and death. Every problem in this world is the effect of man's sin against God. God, being completely righteous and just, could not let this sin go unpunished. So the just and gracious God of the universe sent His only begotten Son, Jesus Christ – God in the flesh – to earth. In a mystery we cannot completely understand, He was 100-percent God and yet 100-percent human. He died on a cross to take the wrath of God upon Himself so people who confess their guilt, turn from their wicked ways, and pursue righteous living might be forgiven and have eternal life with God.

God's just nature demanded a perfect and spotless sacrifice for sin that had to be punished. Jesus was perfect, having never sinned. But He was also "guilty" in the sense that He was human. So His sacrifice appeased the wrath of God by Him being spotless and pure, yet guilty since He represented sinful man.

Jesus came the first time to offer salvation to any person who confesses, repents, and completely trusts who He is and what He accomplished. His desire is for us to become a unique, holy people for His glory. He will come one more time as the eternal judge of all men. He tells us that some will be rewarded with eternal life, but many will be condemned to eternal punishment. Once He renders His final judgement on each of us, there is no "appeal process." Our fate is sealed. He will establish a new heaven and earth where all who have been forgiven of their sins will live eternally in complete peace and joy.

The Bible, the perfect, eternally true Word of God, is simply

the story of God desiring to reconcile sinners to Himself
once again so they might live for eternity with Him.

Once we understand this big-picture view of the Bible, the smaller
pieces come into focus. We better understand what is being taught and
why. And the things we still do not understand we do not worry about
because God will reveal them to us in His perfect timing.

Summary

No church or denomination is perfect. God is always right and every
man or institution is some combination of right and wrong. If you go on
a quest to find a perfect church, you will never find it and will just grow
frustrated and become self-righteous. Since every institution of man
contains error, the key is recognizing if your church or denomination
is trending toward or away from Biblical Christianity. Is it becoming
more like American Christianity with each passing year?

The topics we discussed above and the questions you can respectfully
ask church leaders will help you discern which direction your church
or denomination might be headed. But always remember that we are to
speak the truth in love, always full of grace, and always to help others,
not harm them. Failure to do so makes you part of the problem rather
than part of the solution.

Recent studies by George Barna paint a frightening picture of the
church. For example, a majority of people who call themselves "born-
again believers" believe that Jesus actually sinned while on earth, and
many believe that Satan is a metaphorical symbol rather than an actual
historical figure. An increasing number of professing Christians believe
the biblical account of creation and the flood are allegorical rather than
historic truth. The shocking rise in biblical illiteracy among professing
Christians has become epidemic, leading to serious error in the church,
a membership ill-equipped to spread the gospel and make disciples,
and a growth in church leadership entrenched more in worldly wisdom
than in biblical wisdom.

Next, we look at how to guard our minds and hearts against
deception, and how to help those who are being deceived to confront
and make a decision about their error and worldview. It begins with

differentiating between what God actually says in His Word and how man interprets it incorrectly, either out of ignorance or knowingly and for selfish purposes.

We will now discuss several important principles to help you correctly interpret the Word of God so you will be able to discern deception from truth and lead others to the gospel of reconciliation.

Chapter Three

Knowing How to Spot Truth So You Can Spot Deception

Then Pharisees and scribes came to Jesus from Jerusalem and said, "Why do your disciples break the tradition of the elders? For they do not wash their hands when they eat." He answered them, "And why do you break the commandment of God for the sake of your tradition? You hypocrites! Well did Isaiah prophesy of you, when he said: 'This people honors me with their lips, but their heart is far from me; in vain do they worship me, teaching as doctrines the commandments of men.'" (Matthew 15:1-3, 7-9)

"But woe to you, scribes and Pharisees, hypocrites! For you shut the kingdom of heaven in people's faces. For you neither enter yourselves nor allow those who would enter to go in. Woe to you, scribes and Pharisees, hypocrites! For you travel across sea and land to make a single proselyte, and when he becomes a proselyte, you make him twice as much a child of hell as yourselves." (Matthew 23:13-15)

Do your best to present yourself to God as one approved, a worker who has no need to be ashamed, rightly handling the word of truth. But avoid irreverent babble, for it will lead people into more and more ungodliness, and their talk will spread like gangrene. (2 Timothy 2:15-17)

The Bible tells us that the two things God holds in highest value are His name and His Word. The Pharisees continually tried to put their own spin on the Scriptures to advance their agenda of power. Is the same thing happening in American Christianity? Knowing how to correctly interpret the Word of God is essential to distinguishing between truth and the deception that could cost you your eternal soul. The verses from Timothy tell us that to be approved by God we must rightly handle His Word. But with so many preachers giving their own spin on the Scriptures, how can we know what is correct? *The only way to correctly interpret the Scriptures is to let them interpret themselves.* We will cover four God-given principles that will help us correctly interpret the Bible so we are not easily deceived by people who have mastered how to use it out of context to deceive many.

But first a word of caution. Just because a church may be headed away from Biblical Christianity does not mean that is the intent of church leadership. It is important to understand just how clever and deceptive Satan can be. In the garden of Eden, Adam and Eve were given eternal life, complete dominion, and every good food to eat with only one restriction: to not eat from the Tree of the Knowledge of Good and Evil. Satan managed to twist God's words to them and convinced them to do the one thing that would get them kicked out! With thousands of years to hone his craft of deception, and as the prince of this world, which is becoming more and more evil, Satan wields tremendous influence.

Government, media, and public education (unknowingly, in some instances) support Satan's agenda. This makes evangelism and discipleship even more challenging as the populace is indoctrinated into a faulty thought process that cannot distinguish between truth and deception. So, with perhaps the right heart but faulty logic, the church embarks on a seeker-friendly campaign as part of the Church Growth Movement to attract new members. Subsequently, a growing number of Christian seminaries, where many pastors are trained, start to discount the Bible and elevate "leadership development" in order for the church leaders to act more like CEOs than shepherds tending a flock. And over the course of a decade or two, the church is totally transformed from Biblical Christianity to American Christianity at a rate so slow and subtle that the change is not recognizable to the untrained eye. Like the proverbial frog in a kettle of water being slowly heated to a boiling temperature, we discover too late that the church we have attended for years or decades has abandoned the ways of God for the ways of man.

So if your church is beginning to stray from Biblical Christianity, it is important to determine if this drift is intentional or a mistake that can be rectified by leaders humble enough to seek truth and admit when they are wrong. But to spot error and deception we must know how to interpret the Word of God as God intended it to be understood.

Principle #1: Causality

> "The relationship between something that happens or exists and the thing that causes it; the idea that something can cause another thing to happen or exist."

God established causality to govern His created universe and maintain order. Without it, we would have chaos, and man could never learn and improve upon things, because there would be no patterns indicating why things happen. With causality we experience something (effect) and find reasons and patterns to show why it occurs (source or cause). Understanding and applying causality is the beginning of rational thought. Medical science looks at illnesses (effects) and figures out why these illnesses occur (causes). Once they identify the cause, they can recommend ways people can be healthier by avoiding the cause.

A person can try to treat the effects without addressing the cause, but the bad effects will return. People drink alcohol, use drugs, and take prescription medicine for depression because they are unhappy and think that doing these things will make them happy. But these actions can deepen our depression and become self-made prisons because we treat effects instead of identifying and treating the cause that could lead to a permanent cure. When we can identify the cause of our unhappiness we can correct the root problem without deepening the hole we dig for ourselves. When we understand causality in the Bible we are able to understand why God does what He does.

Do not be deceived: God is not mocked, for whatever one sows, that will he also reap. For the one who sows to his own flesh will from the flesh reap corruption, but the one who sows to the Spirit will from the Spirit reap eternal life. (Galatians 6:7-8)

"For thus says the LORD: When seventy years are completed for Babylon, I will visit you, and I will fulfill to you my promise and bring you back to this place. For I know the plans I have for you, declares the LORD, plans for welfare and not for evil, to give you a future and a hope." (Jeremiah 29:10-11)

These verses point out how important understanding causality is. Many Christians claim Jeremiah 29:11 as their "life verse" and believe it means God will never let them suffer. If they look at verse 11 as a *cause*, they become disillusioned when God disciplines them by allowing trials in their lives. But when we understand causality, we see that verse 11 is the *effect* of verse 10, which is the cause. God had to discipline Israel for their idolatry and disobedience but promised them when His discipline was over, He would restore and heal them. When we hold on to verse 11 as a promised *effect* of God's discipline, we see the value in it and can patiently await His promise.

"And because you listen to these rules and keep and do them, the LORD your God will keep with you the covenant and the steadfast love that he swore to your fathers." (Deuteronomy 7:12)

Cause: Obey God's rules

Effect: God will keep His covenant

And to Adam he said, "Because you have listened to the voice of your wife and have eaten of the tree of which I commanded you, 'You shall not eat of it,' cursed is the ground because of you; in pain you shall eat of it all the days of your life; thorns and thistles it shall bring forth for you; and you shall eat the plants of the field." (Genesis 3:17-18)

Cause: Eating of the Tree of the Knowledge of Good and Evil

Effect: Curses and pain

And he said, "What comes out of a person is what defiles him. For from within, out of the heart of man, come evil thoughts, sexual immorality, theft, murder, adultery, coveting, wickedness, deceit, sensuality, envy, slander, pride, foolishness. All these evil things come from within, and they defile a person." (Mark 7:20-23)

Cause: The evil thoughts of the human heart

Effects: Evil actions

Key points on causality

- Causality is used throughout the Bible.

- Every effect has a cause.

- What a man sows (cause) he will reap (effect).

- Jesus taught that a good cause bears good effects, and a bad cause bears bad effects.

Dangers of not understanding causality in the Bible

- We might begin to believe that we are the instrument of our own salvation instead of God. We might believe that we can initiate salvation through our works (the cause) and that God will then give us the effects (salvation).

- We might begin to believe our righteous deeds are the cause of sanctifying us instead of surrendering and submitting to God's Word and Spirit as the cause of our necessary sanctification. Thinking that we can be the cause of our sanctification can lead to frustration as we continue to fail through our own human efforts. Surrendering to God's Word and Spirit as the cause brings us peace, knowing that

He is working in us and we are not resisting or impeding His work in our lives.

- The prosperity gospel can begin to infiltrate the church, where man is elevated and God is, in essence, lowered to the level of servant if we speak the right words with enough faith. God's will becomes subject to man's will. When God decides to pull the American dream out from under us to discipline our nation for its disobedience, millions will be wondering what else in the Bible cannot be trusted since they were taught that with enough faith God would always provide for our desires of wealth.

Principle #2: Non-contradiction

Jesus said, *"Beware of false prophets, who come to you in sheep's clothing but inwardly are ravenous wolves"* (Matthew 7:15).

If we do not understand non-contradiction, we are vulnerable to false teachers who will deceive us, which could cost us our eternal salvation. Equally important is this: without understanding non-contradiction, we can be led to incorrectly interpret the Word of God, leading us away from God instead of closer to Him.

> *I know that after my departure fierce wolves will come in among you, not sparing the flock; and from among your own selves will arise men speaking twisted things, to draw away the disciples after them.* (Acts 20:29-30)

> *But false prophets also arose among the people, just as there will be false teachers among you, who will secretly bring in destructive heresies, even denying the Master who bought them, bringing upon themselves swift destruction. And many will follow their sensuality, and because of them the way of truth will be blasphemed.* (2 Peter 2:1-2)

Contradictions don't actually exist, conflicts do. I can be both happy and sad (conflicted), but I cannot be both happy and *not* happy at the same time (contradiction). Something or someone cannot be something and *not* be something at the same time. I cannot both believe and *not* believe the same thing at the same time.

There are some mysteries in God's Word that can cause a conflict within us. Which of us can completely understand the nature of the triune God? Which of us can completely reconcile God's sovereignty with man's free will? These are not contradictions; these stem from the fact that we still do not fully understand God in all ways. Understanding the difference between contradiction and conflict is crucial to not being led astray by the many false teachers and false gospels we see today.

Here is another example of the difference between a conflict and a contradiction. The Gospel of John records that Jesus turned water into wine at the wedding feast in Cana, but the other three Gospels do not record this miracle. So we have a conflict, where we wonder why John recorded the event while the other writers did not record it. *This is not a contradiction.* A contradiction would be if John stated, "Jesus turned water into wine at Cana," and another gospel writer said, "Jesus did *not* turn water into wine at Cana."

Because a truth is stated in one part of the Bible but not stated in other parts does not make it a contradiction. But if one book in the Bible states a truth that is directly refuted in another book of the Bible, we would have a contradiction. If one book of the Bible stated, "homosexuality is a sin," but another said, "homosexuality is *not* a sin," we would have a contradiction. Liberals and emergents who believe homosexuality is no longer a sin are in contradiction – and contradiction left unresolved can lead to a worsening thought process to the point they become depraved of mind like Paul spoke of in Romans 1. The Bible contains no contradictions, period. We wrestle with conflicts because of our limited human understanding and wisdom, but nowhere does the Word of God ever contradict itself. *But Christians who do not understand the difference between a conflict and a contradiction are easy prey for false teachers and enemies of the gospel.*

Why is this important? If we believe God contradicts Himself, then we believe God is capable of lying. God says in His Word that He cannot lie. So if we believe God is contradictory, then we really cannot believe anything He says in the Bible.

Just because God said something in the Old Testament that Jesus didn't repeat in the New Testament does not make God contradictory. Jesus is the Word of God *and* God! Failure to understand non-contradiction has fueled the growth of the emergent church movement, leading millions of young professing Christians into heresy and potential eternal damnation if they do not confess and repent. It has fueled the dangerous belief that since Jesus never directly said homosexuality is a sin, it is no longer a sin. This conclusion completely defies logic and rational thought. Jesus had no real reason to overtly state that homosexuality was a sin because everyone already knew it!

Understanding that God cannot contradict Himself is vitally important as we see false prophets and teachers increasing in number. If Jesus had truly contradicted the Father, then Jesus is not God, who is the same yesterday, today, and forever. So the American Christian might believe that either Jesus is not God or that God cannot be trusted because He contradicts Himself.

Summary of Non-Contradiction

- God is a triune God: Father, Son, and Spirit who cannot lie or contradict Himself. He is the same yesterday, today, and forever.

- God's Word, like Him, is non-contradictory and never changes. The New Testament fulfilled the Old Testament, it did not change it.

- If we believe God and His Word are contradictory, we can easily be swayed by false movements and teachers that are on the rise.

Dangers of Failing to Understand Non-Contradiction

- Because Jesus never said the exact words, "homosexuality is still a sin," progressive Christians assume it is now acceptable to God.

- Individual verses can be taken out of context and twisted into dangerous false doctrines when we don't read the Bible in a non-contradictory way. (John 3:16-17 standing on its own is used to support the belief of universal salvation. John 3:18-19 brings the prior two verses into correct context through a biblical conjunctive).

- If you believe God contradicts Himself, then you cannot trust in any of His promises, including salvation through the sacrifice of Jesus.

Principle #3: What is biblical truth?

Then Pilate said to him, "So you are a king?" Jesus answered, "You say that I am a king. For this purpose I was born and for this purpose I have come into the world—to bear witness to the truth. Everyone who is of the truth listens to my voice." Pilate said to him, "What is truth?" After he had said this, he went back outside to the Jews and told them, "I find no guilt in him." (John 18:37-38)

What is your definition of truth? Is it situational or eternal? Do you believe something can be truth today but not be truth tomorrow? Can truth be one thing to you and something different to me?

Conflicting or contradictory definitions for words like *grace, sin,* and *repentance* have damaged the thought processes of individuals and brought confusion and dissent into the church. There is no more important matter facing the Christian church today than correctly defining truth. Is truth objective or subjective? Is truth temporal or eternal? This issue must be addressed if the church is going to do what it is called to do: call men to salvation and sanctification through Jesus Christ alone. *The ability to determine truth objectively in the face of feelings and emotions is what distinguishes people who can spot deception from those deceived by it.*

How do we determine God's intentions for the words He used in the Bible? How do we determine truth? What is the definition of truth?

The way to show yourself approved by God is to correctly interpret the non-contradictory teachings of the Bible. *The Bible, interpreted and understood in a non-contradictory manner, is the only reliable source to interpret itself.* When we use something other than the Bible to interpret it, we are humanists, relying on human understanding in place of God. What does the Bible say about truth?

> *Jesus said to him, "I am the way, and the truth, and the life. No one comes to the Father except through me. If you had known me, you would have known my Father also. From now on you do know him and have seen him."* (John 14:6-7)

The word *truth* in Greek is *aletheia*: "what is true in any matter under consideration." This definition is crucial to understand. It tells us that real truth cannot be contradicted by new information. The truth defined in the Bible is eternal, not subject to flawed human understanding or more information that comes later. Truth is a fact that is eternally right. Only one source can create truth. Truth comes from God alone, the One who knows everything that has existed or ever will exist.

The world cleverly deceives us with statements that sound right but ultimately damage our belief system, values, and thought process. Let's use a recent example of how this deception works. In 2008, Barack Obama ran for president on a platform of "hope and change." Because the majority of Americans operate from a fleshly thought process, he was elected. People knew the system wasn't working but did anyone bother to ask why the system was broken or how it could be fixed? The majority of Americans, including more than half of all professing Christians, voted for him, not knowing the answer to these two questions. Half of all professing Christians elected a president who claimed to be a Christian but supported unrestricted abortion and homosexual marriage, two doctrines God identifies as horrible sins.

Summary on Truth

- The Bible defines truth as a fact that cannot be changed with new information. It is eternal, never changing, and never subjective.

- Since only God knows all things past, present, and future, He can be the only source for truth. In our human understanding we might believe something is truth today but discover later it is not.

- Satan used his opinion, masquerading as truth, to convince Adam and Eve to eat from the Tree of the Knowledge of Good and Evil – the only thing God told them not to do.

- The world presents its opinions as truth to deceive you. American Christianity, by not refuting these tactics and teaching members how to distinguish truth from deception, is feeding into this world's agenda, leading many astray.

- Antichrist, Satan's "perfect" human, will possess the greatest ability to offer deception masqueraded as truth of any man who ever lived. If professing Christians and the world cannot spot deception now, how will they ever be able to spot it in him?

Always remember: God is always 100-percent right and every man or human institution is some combination of right and wrong. Our goal should always be to become more right over time. None of us will attain perfect theology in this life, but our goal is to be humble and become more right over time as God's Word comes into greater focus.

Principle #4: Understanding Biblical Conjunctives

I cannot over-emphasize the importance of understanding biblical conjunctives. I believe they are a representation of what Jesus referred to as the *narrow gate*. Jesus and Paul both taught against two wrong sets of teachers: Judaizers (today's unbiblical legalists) and Gnostics (today's emergents). The legalists add extrabiblical requirements to the gospel while the emergents water down the gospel. The legalists stress strict obedience and restrictions while the emergents stress complete freedom. Some churches lean toward unbiblical legalism, adding to the gospel. Many more are growing into churches with little sound biblical doctrine where professing Christians are held to no standards of belief or behavior. Biblical conjunctives, where a freedom given by

God intersects with a responsibility or restriction, help us walk through the narrow gate. Here is a chart that will be helpful in understanding biblical conjunctives:

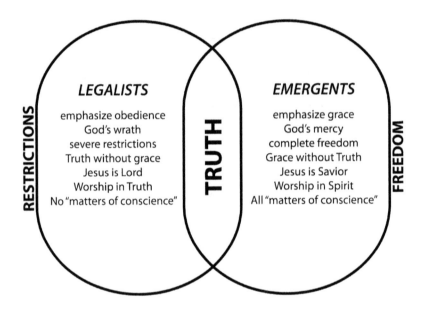

The part where the two circles intersect is where we find biblical truth. Freedoms with responsibilities; obedience to Jesus *with* grace and mercy; truth *and* grace, not one or the other. Understanding the role of God's wrath *and* mercy and who receives which. Jesus as Savior *and* Lord (inseparable). Matters of conscience governed by the clear teachings of Scripture. Christian freedoms set aside for love and the desire to not cause a weaker brother to stumble.

A great exercise is to take the time to look at important doctrines laid out in the Bible and seek the conjunctive – the place where a freedom intersects with a restriction or responsibility toward that freedom. Learning how to use biblical conjunctives will settle many of the arguments Christians have about biblical doctrines. Let's explore some examples of where churches stray because they do not use these God-given principles to accurately handle the Word of God:

What Is the Nature and Character of God?

Concerns: Violating non-contradiction and truth being eternal
This is the single-most important theological issue in the entire Bible. If we get this wrong, it is impossible to get anything of importance correct. God has always existed, He created and sustains all things, and His nature and characteristics never change. He is 100-percent consistent concerning His nature in both the Old and New Testaments. The appearance of Jesus (God in the flesh) did not change God's nature as some progressives claim. God didn't suddenly decide that all was well with sinful man and that He was expecting too much of them. He has always been, and always will be righteous, just, holy, and intolerant of unrepentant sin and sinners.

When you ask church leadership to define the nature of God, you might hear "God is love," citing 1 John 4:8. Respectfully dig deeper, asking the following questions:

- "Does this mean God has ceased to be righteous and just? That His wrath will no longer be poured out on this world?"

- "How do we reconcile God's love with the verses where God says He demands justice and punishment for sin, and where His wrath will one day pour out on all the earth?"

- "If God is love, does that mean everyone will go to heaven? If not, how could a loving God allow anyone to spend eternity in hell?"

If your church is headed toward American Christianity, here are some of the answers they might give:

"God's wrath against sinful man was satisfied by Jesus on the cross." Again, press deeper, asking this: "For all men or is there a qualification?"

They might quote John 3:16 and 17: *"For God so loved the world, that he gave his only Son, that whoever believes in him should not perish but have eternal life. For God did not send his Son into the world to condemn the world, but in order that the world might be saved through him."*

Ask them if those verses mean *all* mankind is now saved. If they answer yes or vacillate, ask them if they can recite the next two verses that follow those: *"Whoever believes in him is not condemned, but whoever does not believe is condemned already, because he has not believed in the name of the only Son of God. And this is the judgment: the light has come into the world, and people loved the darkness rather than the light because their works were evil."*

These verses perfectly represent the need to understand biblical conjunctives, where a freedom God gives intersects with a restriction or requirement for that freedom. *John 3:16-17 is a fact, but not truth.* It only represents the "freedom" part of the conjunctive. John 3:16-19 is truth: it gives the freedom (salvation) and the restriction or requirement (belief and trust in who Jesus is, what He accomplished on the cross, and recognizing Him as Lord over everything).

What Is the Gospel?

Concern: Violation of Biblical Conjunctive on salvation
The gospel being preached these days is increasingly a partial gospel at best, and a complete distortion of God and man's nature at worst. Here is what we covered in chapter 1:

The gospel of salvation has four crucial components:

- **Heartfelt confession:** A person must sincerely admit he is a hopeless, helpless sinner deserving God's wrath and punishment.

- **Heartfelt repentance:** The Bible's definition of repentance is "a change of mind that leads to a consistent change of behavior over time." Man must think differently about the sins he once enjoyed and justified. He must grow to hate them and realize the offense of his sins against a righteous and just God.

- **Complete faith and trust in Jesus Christ alone:** A man must place his complete intellectual and emotional faith in who Jesus Christ is (God in the flesh) and what He accomplished on the cross (He took the wrath of a just God upon Himself in our place). We recognize it is only by God's grace, granted to us through our confession, repentance, and complete faith in Jesus alone, that we are justified by God and brought back into a righteous relationship with Him.

- **Submitting to the lordship of Jesus Christ over all our lives:** This does *not* mean perfect obedience at all times. It *does* mean acknowledging Jesus as Lord and judge over all things and desiring, by the power of God's grace and Spirit, to be continually transformed into the image of Jesus Christ. Increasingly, as we live our lives, our desire is to be more like Jesus in thought, word, and deed.

If any of these points are missing in what we call the gospel, we are believing in an insufficient or false gospel. Here are a few things to listen for to determine the potential direction of your church:

- Is the sinful depravity of unsaved man preached?

- Are we teaching about the continuing wrath of God against unrepentant sinners?

- Is biblical prophecy, particularly the second coming of Jesus, shunned, called unnecessary, or said to be already fulfilled?

- Is *repentance* defined as a change of mind that necessarily leads to a change in behavior over time?

- Are works being added as a condition of salvation (tithing, church attendance, a life of zero sin, feeding the poor, etc.)?

- Is acceptance of Jesus as Lord over all things and our need to submit completely to Him in all matters stressed?

Can Your Church Leadership Distinguish between Clever Deception and Biblical Truth?

Concern: If church leaders cannot spot deception, and you depend on them to interpret truth, your soul may be in jeopardy
Can your church leaders distinguish between a fact and truth? A fact is something believed to be correct in the present but later could be

found wrong as new information is revealed. A truth is eternal and no new information can ever change it.

Fact: Jesus came to the world the first time not to condemn, but to offer forgiveness and salvation to sinful men.

Truth: While His first visit was to offer salvation to repentant sinners, He will return a second time to judge every man with His Word, and many will be condemned to eternal hell because they rejected His message.

Emergent Christians cite a "factual" verse in the Bible and redefine it as "truth."

Behold, this was the guilt of your sister Sodom: she and her daughters had pride, excess of food, and prosperous ease, but did not aid the poor and needy. (Ezekiel 16:49)

Emergent leaders use this single verse to deceive people, claiming this was the primary sin of Sodom instead of the sexual perversion rampant there. But reading the entirety of Ezekiel 16, along with Genesis 19, gives us truth. Sodom was a wicked society, so perverted by sexual sin that the men wanted to have sex with the two angels God sent there to report on their wickedness just before He destroyed the city. Remember, Satan quoted a single verse from the Old Testament to tempt Jesus. Jesus rebuked him with the correct context of the Scriptures. Sometimes the most dangerous deception is taking the Bible out of correct context!

When Jim Wallis of Sojourners was invited to be the keynote speaker at a Christian youth event and we opposed it, the festival organizers asked me to speak to Wallis before making our decision. I spent nearly two hours in conversation with him and what finally revealed his real agenda was his answer when I asked him this question: "What does the world look like just before Jesus' return and what does He do when He returns?" Wallis told me that Jesus could not return until man made the planet pristine once again, free of poverty, pollution, and injustice. Then Jesus would return and rule over a peaceful world. This is the opposite of what the Bible says, where the world will spin into total evil and Jesus returns to judge all men and create a new heaven and earth. But because the majority of pastors in our community valued unity over truth, Wallis was welcomed with open arms by the vast majority of pastors, and hundreds were deceived by his social justice gospel.

Jesus and the letters from the apostles frequently warn the church to recognize dangerous false teachings and expose those who teach them. But American Christianity values a false unity that leads to larger attendance and finances over truth. And when the truth of God is ignored or compromised, the slide toward apostasy is not far away.

Other Signs of Potential Problems

Does your church leadership have a library? Does it contain books from emergent leaders like Jim Wallis, Tony Campolo, Brian McLaren, or Tony Jones? Does it contain "prosperity" books from people like Joel Osteen, Kenneth Copeland, Creflo Dollar, or Benny Hinn?

Can your church leaders biblically address controversial issues facing the church such as social justice, homosexuality, and gender confusion? Are these subjects ever addressed in church sermons, and if so, how are they addressed? Is the approach to people in a sinful lifestyle grace, truth, or both?

Ask which is more important to God: love or truth.

Ask which Jesus considered most important: meeting physical or spiritual needs of people.

Is feeding the poor considered the gospel or an *effect* of the gospel for Christians? Is the mission of the church to reach out to the poor in our community? If so, what are you reaching them with – temporary needs, the gospel, or both? Does your church teach that the Bible says those who will not work should not eat?

Does your church discuss two crucial issues infecting American Christianity: the acceptance of homosexuality and gender confusion? Is homosexuality clearly defined as sin according to God's Word? Does your church teach what the Bible teaches, and credible medical science confirms, that gender is assigned by God at birth and cannot be changed? Or are these issues ignored to avoid controversy? Are you being taught to "just love on them" without speaking the truth? Are church families who are facing these issues in their families being trained how to address them by speaking the truth with grace?

On the other side of the spectrum, is your church speaking out against homosexuality while turning a blind eye to heterosexual sin in the body? Are we teaching what Jesus taught about committing adultery in our hearts with our looks and sexual fantasies toward others?

Are you being taught that while a born-again believer's sins have been forgiven, their sins are still an affront to a holy God? That God will discipline His adopted children for their continuing sin and disobedience? Or is the message that sin is of no more consequence because we have been saved? Are you being taught that your continuing in sin while under grace is bringing shame on the name of the One who died on a cross to save you?

Can You Summarize the Major Points of the Entire Bible in Two Minutes?

Forgive my redundancy here, but this point is so critical that it bears repeating over and over until it is understood. If we do not understand the big picture of God's Word, how can we possibly hope to understand the deep wisdom contained in it? More importantly, in a world where evil is rampant and sin is more and more acceptable, and where people are increasingly preoccupied, the ability to succinctly and effectively communicate the core message of God's Word to sinful man is essential. Too many people attempting to share the gospel get lost in the weeds and dragged into side conversations where they find themselves on the defensive. A short, concise message summarizing the Bible from Genesis 1 to Revelation 22 is crucial to know and communicate these days.

I doubt that if you ask your church leadership to summarize the Bible in a two-minute presentation they will be able to do so right away because they have probably never been asked to do so. So give them grace and allow them time to get back to you on your question. Giving them adequate time to gather their thoughts and make their best case will negate them feeling they are being put on the spot, and their well thought-out answer will give you great information on the direction of your church. Here is how I summarized the Bible in less than two minutes earlier:

God created all things and sustains all things. He has

always existed and will always exist. He is perfect and thus never changes. God created all we see and He created man in His image to take dominion over all things. But man, given a free will to obey or disobey, chose disobedience and rebellion against God. We decided we knew better than Him how things should be run. Man sinned against a holy and perfect God who had given him everything and had put only one restriction on him.

Sin entered the world and because of it, decay, destruction, and death. Every problem in this world is the effect of man's sin against God. God, being completely righteous and just, could not let this sin go unpunished. So the just and gracious God of the universe sent His only begotten Son, Jesus Christ – God in the flesh – to earth. In a mystery we cannot completely understand, He was 100-percent God and yet 100-percent human. He died on a cross to take the wrath of God upon Himself so people who confess their guilt, turn from their wicked ways, and pursue righteous living might be forgiven and have eternal life with God.

God's just nature demanded a perfect and spotless sacrifice for sin that had to be punished. Jesus was perfect, having never sinned. But He was also "guilty" in the sense that He was human. So His sacrifice appeased the wrath of God by Him being spotless and pure, yet guilty since He represented sinful man.

Jesus came the first time to offer salvation to any person who confesses, repents, and completely trusts who He is and what He accomplished. His desire is for us to become a unique, holy people for His glory. He will come one more time as the eternal judge of all men. He tells us that some will be rewarded with eternal life, but many will be condemned to eternal punishment. Once He renders His final judgement on each of us, there is no "appeal process." Our fate is sealed. He will establish a new heaven and earth where all who have been forgiven of their sins will live eternally in complete peace and joy.

The Bible, the perfect, eternally true Word of God, is simply the story of God desiring to reconcile sinners to Himself once again so they might live for eternity with Him.

There is a summary of the entire Bible and the gospel in less than two minutes. It covers creation, sin and the fall, man's inability to be righteous with God again by his own efforts, reconciliation to God through Jesus Christ at His first visit, and His return to judge all men when He comes back, restoring perfection to His creation forever, all without contradiction. If a pastor or preacher cannot give an effective message similar to this, you might be in a church headed toward American Christianity. Even if your church remains solid biblically, the inability to concisely summarize the story of God wanting to reconcile sinful man to Himself renders us ineffective in sharing the gospel message with the lost. But if church leadership leaves out any of the key elements of the creation account, sin, confession, repentance, atonement, requirement for increased holiness, and Jesus' return to judge all men, you have an incomplete story, and the calling or the ability of the teacher can be fairly questioned. Teachers of the Word have a responsibility to teach the full counsel of the Bible and to be able to explain the biblical story effectively.

How Do You Feel after the Sermon Teaching?

Is the sermon an important part of your worship gathering? Or is it overshadowed by the praise and worship singing or other items? My dear friend Elijah Abraham is a former Muslim and now born-again believer who travels around the world equipping pastors and Christians to reach Muslims with the true gospel. He tells me of churches in Africa and Asia where he will go on preaching for four to five hours with the fellowship still wanting more. They often travel by foot ten miles or more to get to church and spend six to seven hours hearing the Word, praying, and glorifying God.

American Christianity, which is consumer centered and not God centered, will cater to our flesh by making sure sermons never exceed thirty minutes so people can get home to the television or other activities. Our preaching has turned into twenty-to-thirty-minute canned presentations where a particular Scripture may make an appearance but is quickly forgotten in a sea of life stories and cute jokes. The Bible verses are conformed more to our lives rather than preached that our lives need to be conformed to God's Word.

Privately some pastors have confessed to me that their sermon preparation consists of going to Rick Warren's *pastors.com* site to cobble together a Scripture or two, surrounded and infused with cute life stories that people relate to. This is sloppy and lazy and might be the effect of church leadership asking the pastor to perform so many other duties (fundraiser, counselor, janitor, office manager) that he has inadequate time to shepherd his family and spend a lot of time in prayer and sermon preparation. The primary duties of a pastor are to preach the Word and equip the saints for the work of the Holy Spirit. If your pastor is more like a CEO, or is also straddled with a myriad of other duties, you have the makings of a very unhealthy church that might be going in the wrong direction. (Asking the elders for a job description for your pastor might be very enlightening.)

When you hear a sermon, what emotions come to your mind? Are you only feeling better about yourself, even your continuing sin? Or do you experience what I refer to as the "paradox of grace"? When I hear a powerful sermon from God's Word about how sin is an affront to Him and how Jesus has called us to be a unique people, pure and spotless (Titus 2), my initial reaction is deep sorrow and repentance because of the sin I continue to commit. I see His holiness and my continuing sin and I am heartbroken. But then I hear how Jesus took the punishment for my sins upon Himself and that I am forgiven. And I am left with the joy of His grace, love, and forgiveness, but am challenged all the more to stop sinning and bringing shame on His holy name, leading me to deeper holiness. If you do not feel some guilt and shame from your ongoing sin from the sermon message, something crucial is missing – a call to holiness.

Does Your Church Stress Vision and Mission?

Vision and mission statements are all the rage in American Christianity, spearheaded by Rick Warren's Purpose Driven Church model. Is there anything wrong with a church having a vision or mission? Not necessarily, except that Jesus already gave us the church's vision and mission:

> And Jesus came and said to them, "All authority in heaven and on earth has been given to me. Go therefore and make disciples of all nations, baptizing them in the name of the Father and of the Son and of the Holy Spirit, teaching them to observe all that I have commanded you. And behold, I am with you always, to the end of the age." (Matthew 28:18-20)

It is always in our sinful human nature to think that we can improve on something God has done or given us. Adam and Eve were given paradise but couldn't resist the temptation to make it better. Jesus gave us the gospel of reconciliation, which requires man to acknowledge his sinful nature, but somehow American Christianity thinks it can improve the gospel by making it more inclusive through fewer restrictions. The same goes for when a church decides it needs to fashion a vision or mission statement when Jesus already gave it to us just before He ascended into heaven.

As we discussed in an earlier chapter, there is a difference between conscious (purposeful) sin and unconscious (out of ignorance) sin. I believe in the vast majority of cases with churches enamored with vision statements it is unconscious sin. It stems back to the implementation of the Church Growth Movement inspired by Peter Drucker and accepted by Rick Warren and Bill Hybels. Apparently, in their minds, God's way of growing the church is inadequate.

If your church is touting its vision and mission statements, ask your church leaders if they believe Jesus already gave the church a vision and a mission. Their answer will give you clues as to their thought process and intent.

- How Is Sin Addressed in the Church?

- Is Church Discipline Used When Biblically Called For?

The Church Growth Movement stresses quantity over quality. It is more interested in the number of people in the church than in the church's depth of spiritual maturity. The simplest way to grow the church is to lower the standards of membership. And the easiest way to lower the standards is to disregard sin and accept it, or even worse, justify it.

There may be no single greater threat to the purity and effectiveness of the church than its failure to correctly implement church discipline. But before we start out on witch hunts, we must clearly differentiate between repentant sin and unrepentant sin. Every member of every Christian church since the time of Jesus has contained sinners; we all fall far short of the glory and righteousness of God. Yes, the church is a gathering of sinners. But the church is meant to be a fellowship of *repentant* sinners, acknowledging the ongoing sin we struggle to overcome, and willing to be held accountable and disciplined when necessary. This is how a Biblical church functions.

American Christian churches avoid discussing sin, often eliminating it from the gospel presentation, and certainly never daring to confront a church member when he is living in unrepentant sin. Why? Because many professing Christians have fallen for the lie that salvation does not come with a responsibility: the responsibility to pursue a holy life through God's Word and Spirit. They have been lulled into a false sense of eternal security by a false gospel that does not show us our sinful depravity and the Bible's requirements to be purified and made holy as a result of God's grace. To suddenly start preaching about ongoing sin and the need for church discipline would send a majority of American Christians out the door to find a church that continues to justify their sins and feed their flesh. And since American Christianity's success is built on nickels and noses, the pastor would be fired and replaced with a CEO who could rebuild the business back to its former size and prominence.

> It is actually reported that there is sexual immorality among you, and of a kind that is not tolerated even among pagans, for a man has his father's wife. And you are arrogant! Ought you not rather to mourn? Let him who has done this be removed from among you.

For though absent in body, I am present in spirit; and as if present, I have already pronounced judgment on the one who did such a thing. When you are assembled in the name of the Lord Jesus and my spirit is present, with the power of our Lord Jesus, you are to deliver this man to Satan for the destruction of the flesh, so that his spirit may be saved in the day of the Lord.

Your boasting is not good. Do you not know that a little leaven leavens the whole lump? Cleanse out the old leaven that you may be a new lump, as you really are unleavened. For Christ, our Passover lamb, has been sacrificed. Let us therefore celebrate the festival, not with the old leaven, the leaven of malice and evil, but with the unleavened bread of sincerity and truth.

I wrote to you in my letter not to associate with sexually immoral people—not at all meaning the sexually immoral of this world, or the greedy and swindlers, or idolaters, since then you would need to go out of the world. But now I am writing to you not to associate with anyone who bears the name of brother if he is guilty of sexual immorality or greed, or is an idolater, reviler, drunkard, or swindler—not even to eat with such a one. (1 Corinthians 5:1-11)

Look at the important things Paul is saying in these verses:

- The church was tolerating behavior even pagans would not tolerate and was arrogant about it.

- The unrepentant sinner was to be judged as an unbeliever and thrown out of the church for their benefit and his.

- There was to be no Christian fellowship with this unrepentant sinner until he confessed and repented because he claimed to be a brother in the faith.

- Unrepentant sinners claiming to be Christians who are greedy, sexually immoral, idolaters, financially dishonest, or drunkards should be dealt with in the same manner.

Allow me to again make this very important point: It is important to differentiate between one who has repented of these sins but still struggles in these areas and the professing Christian who has not changed his mind (repented) about these sins and justifies them with his own human understanding. The church should be a place of repentant sinners striving by God's grace to be increasingly purified. It should never encourage unrepentant sinners to remain that way because it gives them a false sense of salvation and could spread like a cancer throughout the church itself.

The recent events with Pastor Bill Hybels and Willow Creek Church exemplify the damage done when church leadership does not exercise correct church discipline. When Hybels was accused of several sexual improprieties, the elders first defended him, discrediting the accusers. A couple months later they resigned, admitting they had failed in several ways. Now Willow Creek is doing damage control and trying to maintain their megachurch status. And guess what? They will, because a majority of their members have already been indoctrinated into American Christianity. This will be looked at as a sad single event instead of a colossal failure of church leadership to exercise boundaries, accountability, and discipline – the very things American Christians do not want in their own lives.

Discovering how your church addresses the doctrine of church discipline is important in determining the direction of your church. Is there a biblical plan for church discipline? Are church members and leaders held accountable for their lives as Christians? If your church dismisses the importance of church discipline and is not prepared with a biblical answer to hypothetical situations, you may have a church leaning toward American Christianity. Jesus gave us the model for church discipline:

> *"If your brother sins against you, go and tell him his fault,*
> *between you and him alone. If he listens to you, you have*
> *gained your brother. But if he does not listen, take one or two*
> *others along with you, that every charge may be established*
> *by the evidence of two or three witnesses. If he refuses to*
> *listen to them, tell it to the church. And if he refuses to listen*

even to the church, let him be to you as a Gentile and a tax collector." (Matthew 18:15-17)

American Christianity discounts this as a message solely of settling disputes between believers. But a clear understanding speaks to the need for church discipline in the final verse. American Christianity values numbers over quality and will do all it can to keep as many members as possible. Biblical Christianity understands the importance of church discipline for the church and the professing believer.

What Does Your Church Teach about Christians Judging Others?

I am not a fan of "life verses" many Christians identify themselves with. Some Christians often cite their life verse as Jeremiah 29:11: *For I know the plans I have for you, declares the LORD, plans for welfare and not for evil, to give you a future and a hope.*

It has been used to justify the Word of Faith movement's false gospel and agenda, and has led many Christians into a false belief that God will never discipline them or allow trials in their lives. But when we read the preceding verse and those immediately following it, we get the entire picture:

> *"For thus says the LORD: When seventy years are completed for Babylon, I will visit you, and I will fulfill to you my promise and bring you back to this place."* (Jeremiah 29:10)

> *"Then you will call upon me and come and pray to me, and I will hear you. You will seek me and find me, when you seek me with all your heart. I will be found by you, declares the LORD, and I will restore your fortunes and gather you from all the nations and all the places where I have driven you, declares the LORD, and I will bring you back to the place from which I sent you into exile."* (Jeremiah 29:12-14)

So God's message in correct context is this: "I love you, but when you stray into disobedience I will discipline you to teach you. And when you reach out to Me in prayer and humility, I will end your trials in My perfect timing and restore you." The life verses for American Christianity are probably these:

"Judge not, that you be not judged." (Matthew 7:1)

"If anyone hears my words and does not keep them, I do not judge him; for I did not come to judge the world but to save the world." (John 12:47)

This is the problem when we teach snippets out of the Bible instead of slowing down and teaching it in complete context: We develop false and dangerous theology. In the verses right after Matthew 7:1 Jesus goes on to tell us how we *should* judge others effectively for their benefit! And look at the verse immediately after John 12:47: *"The one who rejects me and does not receive my words has a judge; the word that I have spoken will judge him on the last day."*

At a time when the world desperately needs the grace and truth of Jesus Christ, American Christianity, selling out to nickels and noses, hides behind a false doctrine by taking two Bible verses out of context. Because if we sound judgmental to the world, they won't want to come to our churches, and if we dare teach Christians how to biblically judge one another, those in our church will feel uncomfortable and leave. These are both viewed as serious impediments to church growth. So a great question you can respectfully ask your church leadership is this: "What does the Bible teach us about Jesus and Christians judging others?" The Bible is very clear about this subject:

- The first time Jesus came He did not come to judge the world but to offer it a way out of God's wrath and judgment. But the second time He comes He will judge all men with His Word as the instrument of judgment. Truly born-again believers will be rewarded with eternal life with God. All others will be cast into eternal hell.

- Christians should not bother judging the world at this time. We will judge the world, and angels, when we are with Christ (1 Corinthians 6:1-4).

- Christians are not qualified to judge or determine the

eternal destination of any person. Only God, who is perfectly righteous, just, and all knowing, is qualified to make that judgment.

- Christians *are* to judge the fruits (beliefs, words, and actions) of professing believers for their benefit.

Because of laziness in how many approach the Word of God, we have been confused on this important subject. The word used for *judge* in the New Testament is one of two words with different meanings in the original language:

Krino: "to try, condemn, and punish"

Anakrino: "scrutinize, investigate, and discern"

God is the only one righteous and just enough to proclaim *krino* judgment on the eternal soul of man, and the only one qualified to condemn and punish man in hell. Believers are to *anakrino* one another, judging if our actions match up with our stated beliefs. We should always do this for the benefit of the other person, to help them see their contradiction and sin and grow in holiness. If your church's stance is something like "Jesus never judged others so neither should we," you are hip-deep in American Christianity. And if you are in a Biblical Christian church, understanding the correct role and context of judging others will help the church stay on the narrow path, teaching, correcting, and rebuking others for their benefit.

Summary

No Christian or church is perfect. Perfection will not be attained until Jesus completes the work He has begun in us and in His eternal bride, the church. But the Bible tells us to pursue holiness by the power of God's Word and Spirit within us. Salvation is not the end of our journey; it is the first step on a journey to holiness through sanctification. But much of American Christianity presents salvation as the journey's end instead of the first step toward holy perfection as the eternal bride of Christ.

Understand that if your church is trending toward American Christianity it might not be your pastor's fault. Whom did he learn under? What does his church leadership lay out as his duties and calling?

Is he only giving the church members what they want (mushy teaching that does not convict) because his family's livelihood is dependent on what the church pays him? These are not excuses, just the reality we face in this era of consumer-driven churches.

Give your church leadership the opportunity to answer the questions laid out in this book so you can discern which direction the church might be headed. But be patient and graceful rather than prideful and accusatory. It is only the grace of God that opens our eyes to truth. Here is a summary of the questions and topics you can discuss with your church's leadership that will give some insight on the direction your church might be headed.

- What is the nature and character of God?

- What is the gospel?

- Can your church leadership distinguish between clever deception and biblical truth?

- Can you summarize the major points of the entire Bible in two minutes?

- How long does the sermon last and how much of the Bible is used in sermon teachings?

- Does your church stress vision and mission?

- How is sin addressed in the church? Is church discipline used when necessary?

- What does your church teach about Christians judging others?

Just because your church may fail in answering one or two of these questions might not necessarily mean they are on the wrong path. But that may be an indication that all is not well theologically and that trouble is on the horizon. Most importantly, the way they respond to your sincere, grace-filled questions might give you an indication as to whether your church leadership is immersed in pride and self-righteousness or if it is humble and willing to grow in the knowledge and grace of Jesus Christ. It will expose their hearts and true motives. Are they humble and willing to change their minds if the Bible proves they are wrong? Or will they double down and pull rank?

The only way to spot clever deception is to know the truth and trust fully in it. Over the past several decades American Christianity has infiltrated many formerly solid churches. As the growth in member numbers became more important that the spiritual growth and depth of members, many churches have compromised on God's Word because its message was viewed as too harsh to attract new church members. This has coincided with a growing number of Christian seminaries emphasizing leadership development over biblical knowledge and wisdom for the pastors educated there. God's Word is even being discredited within many churches as the biblical creation account and the nature and character of God are being questioned more and more in professing Christian churches.

It is time for every church leadership team to make a decision. They either commit to interpreting the Bible as God intended us to and stand firmly upon it as eternal, uncompromising truth, or they decide to rely on their own human understanding, which comes with the baggage of our continuing sinful nature. And they owe it to their members to be open and honest about the direction they choose. Is the Bible eternally true and sufficient in all important matters? Or does it require modernization with an influx of human "wisdom" like the emergents and lukewarm Christians believe?

One more factor is really starting to come to the foreground. The hatred of God and Christians is reaching a fever pitch in our nation as education, media, and government unknowingly carry out the wishes of the father of lies.

Even churches who remain as solid Biblical churches will be challenged and threatened in ways they cannot imagine in the coming years. They will be forced to compromise biblical principles or risk being shut down. It is imperative for these remaining solid churches to understand what is going on around them and begin to prepare for the day when they might be forced underground. Next, we will look at the tactics the enemy is using to discredit and threaten the church and how we can prepare for those attacks.

Chapter Four

The Biblical Church's Battle
for Influence and Survival

The most successful military campaigns are conducted by forces that are a combination of troops directly involved in the battle and subversives seeking to weaken the opponent from within. We will look at both components, starting with institutions directly involved in a full frontal assault on the church in America. I will give a brief summary on these, as I covered them extensively in my two previous books.

Public Education

John Dewey, considered the "Father of American Education," was an avowed Marxist and humanist, journeying to the Soviet Union to learn how Communists indoctrinated children into their ungodly system. Lenin famously wrote, "Give me four years to teach the children and the seed I have sown will never be uprooted." Because of Dewey's passion and the ongoing powerful lobbying influence of the National Education Association, our children now go through twelve-plus years of indoctrination where they are no longer taught *how* to think, but rather *what* to think. Recent studies show that more than 70 percent of young people support socialism, a godless form of government, so the indoctrination has definitely taken root.

Prayer, and ultimately God, was thrown out of public education in 1963. The secular government mandates evolution rather than biblical creationism be taught as truth. And under President Obama, every public school has been threatened with a withholding of tax dollars if they do not accommodate students who are confused about their gender.

School districts around the nation are actually implementing policies that not only intentionally confuse young children about their gender, but also prohibit parents from learning about how their children are being confused, manipulated, and deceived.

Media

Up until the late 1960s, television news shows had to distinctly identify when they were reporting facts and when they were inserting their own opinions (commentary). Because the public education system has indoctrinated the American public through the Soviet Union model, most Americans cannot distinguish between news and commentary, facts and opinions, or truth and deception anymore. We just go along with whatever our favorite news outlet presents as truth. Here is an example of the media misrepresenting opinion as fact:

Fact: Thousands of Americans lost their lives in the war against Iraq.

Opinion: Thousands of Americans lost their lives in an *unjust* war in Iraq.

Since the public education system has done such an excellent job of diminishing the ability of students to think rationally, many adults these days cannot distinguish between facts and opinions, which becomes a useful tool to indoctrinate people into deception that is now well entrenched in our culture. Everyone has the right to their opinion about whether a war is justified or not, but presenting opinion as truth to an unsuspecting audience is journalistic malpractice.

Government

Slowly, the United States has transitioned from a form of government that serves people to one which the people must serve or risk losing the financial handouts the government made necessary through massive taxation to fund social justice programs, bureaucratic waste, and excessive lifestyles of politicians. Religious freedom is disappearing, sacrificed at the altar of political correctness and powerful lobby groups like the LGBTQ movement, which has successfully categorized anyone who disagrees with their agenda as racist, homophobic, or misogynistic.

Make no mistake, this is a powerful "axis of evil" that supports the agenda of the father of lies, doing his bidding in the name of fairness and equality. But with all its might and influence, will it be able to conquer the true church?

> *"And I tell you, you are Peter, and on this rock I will build my church, and the gates of hell shall not prevail against it. I will give you the keys of the kingdom of heaven, and whatever you bind on earth shall be bound in heaven, and whatever you loose on earth shall be loosed in heaven."*
> (Matthew 16:18-19)

Jesus as God knows the future and cannot lie, so the enemy will never subdue the true church. So if the prevailing church in America *is* being subdued through infestation from secular humanism, teaching the doctrines of men as if they were of God, what does that tell us? That American Christianity is a fake Christianity.

The Infestation of Humanism into the Church

According to Gallup research, in 1996 only 27 percent of Americans believed homosexual marriage should be legal, while 68 percent opposed it. By 2018 those numbers were completely reversed: now 67 percent approve of homosexual marriage while only 31 percent still oppose it (*www.news.gallup.com/poll/1651/gay-lesbian-rights.aspx*). A recent study shows 69 percent of people believe that people struggling with gender identity should be provided with surgeries so their physical bodies match their perceived gender (*www.globalnews.ca/news/3991849/transgender-people-world-accepting-ipsos-poll*). According to a recent poll by the Pew Research Center, 35 percent of professing Christians believe that the gender God gave people at birth can be changed if they so desire. So if church growth is your "god," even mentioning these controversial topics from the pulpit could cause a mass exodus from your church, setting you back financially. This is what happens when we redefine what church success looks like, from people growing in holiness to nickels and noses.

One has to wonder how Christians could be seduced by lies like this, but a study by Barna Group gives us a clue. The study conducted back in 2004 showed only half of Protestant pastors had a biblical worldview. So over the past fifteen years, half of Protestant church members heard sermons from a person who did not hold a biblical worldview.

A person's worldview can be generally summarized by answering one basic question: Is mankind at its nature evil or good? The Bible clearly says that every way and thought of man is evil to its core. The secular humanist worldview is that man is in essence good and can get better, making the world better as we live and apply human reasoning. In other words, half of Protestant pastors back in 2004 thought man could improve on God's ways. This is the primary reason American Christianity is spreading through our churches, and we are starting to see the trickle-down effect in what professing Christians believe about truth.

A 2017 study by Barna Group shows how this secularist human world-view is infecting the church (*www.onenewsnow.com/church/2017/05/30/ barna-hodge-podge-of-beliefs-among-born-agains*). These were the opinions of people who identified themselves as born-again believers:

- 24 percent believe the Bible contains errors.

- 34 percent do not believe the creation account in Genesis.

- 36 percent believe the Bible is not accurate regarding principles it teaches.

- 42 percent believe Satan is a fictitious character.

- 48 percent believe Jesus sinned while on earth.

- 57 percent believe the Holy Spirit is merely symbolic, not real.

- 63 percent believe a person's good works can earn them heaven.

- 75 percent believe people are basically good.

If self-professed believers look at God and His Word this way, imagine how most Americans look at them. Given the big picture of these findings, there is a strong possibility that many of the people you attend church with, and perhaps even your church leadership, have a secular worldview and not a biblical one. Your church may be selling out to American Christianity. And while there is hope that these church leaders can see the error of their ways and humbly repent and change the direction of their church, there is one other worldly factor that might dissuade them from doing so.

The Coming Persecution of Faithful Christians in America

Our Christian brothers and sisters in places like China, Pakistan, and Iran face persecution we know little about here in America. Our current idea of persecution is when we are belittled on social media over our biblical worldview and beliefs. But that is changing, and real persecution may come very rapidly in the next few years. Several court cases and new legislation restricting religious freedoms, combined with a growing hatred of God and His people, are forming a "perfect storm" that could hit the church in America very shortly.

Note the words "Faithful Christians" above. American Christianity is not threatened by the plans of the enemy because it is already compromising, putting itself into position to survive real persecution. Just like the Catholic and Protestant churches in Nazi Germany who gave in to Hitler and supported his rise to power, American Christianity churches will support anything that allows them to continue to run their business, including compromising biblical truth for human doctrines that contradict God's Word. They will submit to man instead of God for the sake of survival, unlike the true Christian martyrs dying around the world every day.

There is a well-planned pattern in Satan's attempt to discredit the church and lead people astray. It starts with something that sounds right but is deceptive, taking hold because we are increasingly ignorant of God's Word or consciously choosing to disobey it. There is a five-step process to the enemy's plan to discredit the church and render her ineffective:

- Creating doubt about truth

- Softening the church's resistance to this world by preaching unity and tolerance for anything

- Mocking, intimidating, and threatening Christians into silence and acceptance of their agenda

- Restricting the church to its four walls and eliminating its influence on society

- All-out persecution where Christians are identified as a serious threat to society

Step 1: Create doubt about truth

The first part of this step is to get Christians so preoccupied with pursuing the things of this life (money, social media, entertainment) that they just don't have time for serious study of God's Word. This forces them to trust in those who claim to understand God's Word because of a seminary degree or the title of *pastor* or *preacher*. But because we have become lazy in our reading and understanding of the Bible, we can be easily deceived by an eloquent speaker or a leader with a title.

Increasing ignorance of God's Word leads to the second part of this strategy: redefining God. To some who value money as their true god, the Bible becomes all about what God can do for them: giving them wealth, prosperity, and health, instead of being about sinful man becoming reconciled to a holy God through surrender and obedience. Feeding right in to our desires for wealth, the prosperity gospel replaces the gospel of reconciliation as the roles of servant and master are reversed.

With younger people, who are by nature rebellious against the prior generation, social justice has replaced the pursuit of wealth as their passion. But being the crafty veteran deceiver that he is, Satan replaces biblical justice with human social justice that subtly but effectively redefines the gospel, making it all about the collective works of man instead of the perfectly timed justice of God. American Christianity has become infused with prosperity preachers, social justice advocates, and self-professed Christians who doubt the creation account in

Genesis, doubt the truth of a worldwide flood, and now even refer to the Bible as "outdated" and unable to anticipate modern problems like gender confusion and abortion. And because our study of God's Word ranks much lower on our priority list than football, entertainment, or the pursuit of wealth, we take the easy way and just trust anything a person in authority says about the Bible. We attempt to reconcile God more into what we think He *should* be instead of allowing God's Word and Spirit to reconcile us to Himself. We insist that God compromise His eternal nature and character rather than us submitting to Him.

When you look at the varying denominations and how they are split on issues such as abortion, homosexuality, and gender confusion, it is obvious that there is a "truth gap" in American Christianity. Our inability to discern deception from truth has us fragmented on important doctrinal issues. But the enemy addresses that in step 2 of his plan:

Step 2: Preach the need for unity and tolerance in the church, and attack anyone who disagrees with church leadership

> But you must remember, beloved, the predictions of the apostles of our Lord Jesus Christ. They said to you, "In the last time there will be scoffers, following their own ungodly passions." It is these who cause divisions, worldly people, devoid of the Spirit. (Jude 1:17-19)

The success of public education and media in diminishing the ability of people to think rationally and logically, combined with growing numbers of church leadership who refuse to be held accountable to the Bible, have led to confusion about who the dividers in the church really are. These verses in Jude clearly state that those who bring in false doctrines are the dividers. But today, those who question false doctrines creeping into the church are labeled as dividers.

> Then Pharisees and scribes came to Jesus from Jerusalem and said, "Why do your disciples break the tradition of the elders? For they do not wash their hands when they eat." He answered them, "And why do you break the commandment of God for the sake of your tradition? You hypocrites! Well

did Isaiah prophesy of you, when he said: 'This people hon-
ors me with their lips, but their heart is far from me; in vain
do they worship me, teaching as doctrines the command-
ments of men.'" (Matthew 15:1-3, 7-9)

Just as in Jesus' time, many of the religious leaders in American Christianity have distorted the Scriptures to the point that the doctrines of men are increasingly taught as the doctrines of the Bible.

This toxic combination of church leaders elevating the wisdom of men over God's Word, along with faithful Christians who stand against false doctrine and teachers being chastised as dividers, is fundamental to the growth of American Christianity. It is the exact opposite of Biblical Christianity where the Word of God is superior to the teachings of men and Christians are called to hold one another accountable to become a pure, spotless church for the glory of God.

Every time a Christian man or woman of courage dares to address wrong doctrine or beliefs creeping into the church, they are sure to be met with a chastising word about how Jesus values church unity above all things and that we are never supposed to judge another person. For the past eight years I have been warning listeners to our show about the dangers of the Church Growth Movement that Peter Drucker introduced to Bill Hybels and Willow Creek Church. When Drucker convinced Hybels, Rick Warren, and others that the way to grow the church was to run it like a business, giving the customers what they want, everything started to change. We have witnessed attempts to blur the lines between Biblical Christianity and Islam, to elevate secular humanists as leaders Christians should emulate, and we have seen the ultimate demise of Hybels due to sexual improprieties that the Willow Creek board initially dismissed and tried to cover up.

Yet pastors would confront me on the issue saying we had no right to judge Willow Creek's fruit and accusing us of dividing the church. We were called Pharisees, when in reality these pastors fit the classical definition of why Jesus chastised the Pharisees of His time: for their hypocrisy and teaching the doctrines of men as if they were from God.

Controlling, Rather Than Feeding the Sheep

A growing number of larger churches have adopted a "small group model" for church members. And while a group of believers gathering to pray and study God's Word can be a very good thing, many wonder if the small group model presented by these large churches is more about controlling church members than encouraging them to grow in the knowledge and grace of Jesus Christ. I have spoken with many solid Christian men and women who have led small groups in their church, only to be chastised by church leadership if they deviated from "the plan."

Many churches have adopted Rick Warren's *Purpose Driven Church* book as the model for small groups within the church. My friend Eric Barger of Take a Stand Ministries has studied the Church Growth Movement and Warren's Purpose Driven Church extensively. Eric documents the connection between Warren and Dan Southerland of Church Transitions Inc. and the dangers of this movement:

> Changing a church from traditional Bible teaching to the Purpose Driven approach isn't always so easy. This is especially so with many Evangelicals who have more awareness of the Scriptures. But Rick Warren, as capable as he may be at convincing pastors to forsake their old ways for the greener pastures of Purpose Driven, does have other outside help in accomplishing the task. Enter one Dan Southerland, the founder of Church Transitions Inc.
>
> The Church Transitions Inc. website boasts that he and his associates have led thousands of churches to transition to the Purpose Driven model. Southerland's bio states that he has trained over 100,000 pastors on how to change existing churches into Purpose Driven churches. . . . For the past seven years he has also been a regular speaker at Rick Warren's own Purpose Driven Church Conference held at Saddleback. According to the Church Transitions Inc. website, half of the events they take part in each year are actually co-sponsored by Warren's Purpose Driven Ministries.
>
> Southerland's book, *Transitioning: Leading Your Church*

Through Change, is promoted and sold through Rick Warren's pastors.com website. In the book, Southerland outlines the plan to bring a church into the Purpose Driven camp. Chapter six is relevant to our discussion here. It's aptly titled: "Dealing with Opposition."

On page 116 of *Transitioning* Dan Southerland states: *"We have experienced two major sources of criticism during our transitions. The first is Christians from more traditional backgrounds. They sometimes struggle with transitions in the church. Not all of our traditional backgrounded Christians have been critical – just the ornery ones. Our second source of criticism is traditional church pastors. Again, not all traditional church pastors – just the meaner ones. I believe that is because they do not understand what we are doing. I hope it is not out of jealousy of our results...."* It isn't brain surgery to correlate this statement with Warren's recent and repeated statements about getting rid of troublemakers (see "Handling Disunity Rick Warren's Way"). By the way Dan, if I have a choice between "results" or standing for Biblical truth, guess what's most important to me?

The Church Transition Inc. website states "We teach a process for leading change that is biblical – based on the book of Nehemiah." Dan Southerland's book repeats this theme as well. On page 115 Southerland writes of Nehemiah's evil adversary, Sanballat, likening him to Purpose Driven opponents in our day.

"If you have read Nehemiah recently, you will remember that Sanballat is Nehemiah's greatest critic and number one enemy. Let me put it plainer than that. Sanballat is a leader from hell. We all have some Sanballats in our churches. This is the guy who opposes whatever you propose.... You cannot call this guy a leader from hell to his face – but you could call him Sanballat."

Think carefully about what is being said in that statement. Southerland is encouraging pastors to think of those who may be their brother or sister in Christ as actually "leaders from hell"! Why? Because they question the validity of a church growth program which lacks Scriptural basis to support it. . . .

So, let's get this straight. According to Church Transitions' Dan Southerland in a book endorsed and sold by Rick Warren, Purpose Driven opposers are equated to filthy, demonic, unbelieving pagans – which is exactly what the real Sanballat actually was. I think we've discovered a new depth to which the Purpose Driven proponents will stoop in order to have it their way. I wonder what lengths will they go to next?

Understand the toxic combination present in churches who adopt the Church Growth model while they are staffed with leaders who will not tolerate anyone questioning their methods. The church is committed to growing by any means necessary, including disregarding biblical doctrine, and if a member of that church dares question the motives or methods of that church's leadership, he is considered a "leader from hell." As secular culture and government applies more and more pressure to churches to conform to humanist philosophy, including radical tolerance for all views, these churches will comply in order to protect their financial status. Since anyone who dares oppose the program of the church will be demonized, there will be few people with the courage to speak out, reinforcing the "herd" mentality of naïve professing Christians in the church who blindly follow leadership right over the spiritual cliff. The church is committed to American Christianity instead of Biblical Christianity, and the slide to full-blown apostasy is well underway.

I have witnessed solid Christians whom I have known for years kicked off elder boards and told they could not even do a Bible study with other believers unless the church controlled the agenda. One pastor told me in confidence that he expressed concerns to his elders about them adopting the Church Growth model and was told to comply, and that if he ever shared his concerns with anyone, they would fire him and make sure he never got another position as pastor. They would tell the next church that considered hiring him that he was an insubordinate troublemaker who would undermine church leadership.

Tolerance of sin for the sake of growth. Valuing unity over truth. Leaders who are unwilling to be challenged when they are leading the church into dangerous waters. This is a toxic combination and a sure sign your church is an American Christianity church and is headed to apostasy.

Now that the enemy has successfully weakened any resistance from within the church that threatens his plan to undermine Biblical Christianity in America, his external forces begin their full frontal attack against the church.

Step 3: Mock, intimidate, and threaten Christians into silence and acceptance of the secular agenda

Barack Obama cited "backwards people" who cling to their Bibles and guns as a threat to America. When running for president in 2016, Hillary Clinton said half of the people who supported Donald Trump are "deplorables." Joe Biden, preparing for a run for president in 2020, recently referred to people who disagree with the LGBTQ movement as "forces of intolerance" and "dregs of society."

Jack Phillips, a Christian cake baker in Colorado, knows how powerful the combination of the LGBTQ movement and a government hostile to religious conscience can be to one's livelihood. And while Phillips was victorious in his battle against the LGBTQ and the Colorado Civil Rights Commission in their attempts to force him to violate his religious convictions, it is important to understand the reasoning behind the Supreme Court's decision. Was it truly a victory for religious freedom? Or a subtle sign to secularists on how to be victorious in the next battle they fight to eliminate religious freedom?

The chief justice of the Supreme Court, John Roberts, seems to value unity over truth (sound familiar?) As records of the Supreme Court's deliberations come into the public light, we discover that Roberts was concerned about the possibility of a narrow decision from the court, so he convinced his fellow judges to narrow the scope of the ruling so they could avoid a 5-4 decision in favor of more unity. The court ruled 7-2 in favor of Phillips, but it is a tainted victory when you understand the rationale for the decision. The court had an opportunity once and for all to determine that the religious conscience of an individual protected him from doing something that violated that conscience. But instead of firmly ruling that the Colorado Civil Rights Commission had no business interfering with Phillips' religious conscience, the ruling criticized the commission's attitude toward Phillips more than their forcing him to comply with their findings. In other words, the court did not rebuff what Colorado did but rather the tone in which they did it. They were "too mean" to Phillips.

What is the result of this spineless ruling that could have once and for all reinforced the freedom of religious expression and conscience? The Colorado commission is badgering and threatening Phillips all over again for a similar situation. While most Christians applauded the Supreme Court's ruling, legal experts and people who see the big picture realize that the Supreme Court actually encouraged continued discrimination against people of religious conscience, lacking the courage to take a firm stand once and for all. Liberals were handed a blueprint for future success in shutting up Christians: at least *publicly pretend* to consider a person's religious conscience before you pursue any means to put them out of business for their "intolerance."

Banning the Bible?

The state of California is poised to pass legislation that would ban the sale of any book that claims homosexuality or transgenderism is wrong or harmful and can be addressed through "reparative therapy." In other words, any book that criticizes these movements or suggests a way out of these dangerous lifestyles would not able to be sold or purchased. Offenders would be subject to severe fines and even potential jail time.

Across our nation courts are ruling that students cannot pray at school events and that teachers cannot even bring a Bible to school to read on their breaks because these actions make others feel uncomfortable. Citizens who dare hold a Bible study in their private homes are being threatened with citations for violating parking restrictions or for meeting without a permit.

So the stage has been set and Christians have been warned. There is a cost to going public with your beliefs. You can expect aggressive resistance with a price to pay if you persist in expressing your religious beliefs. This sets us up for the next step toward religious persecution in America.

Step 4: Restrict the church's sphere of influence to its own four walls

Freedom of Religious Expression versus "Freedom of Worship"

The First Amendment to the U.S. Constitution is clear about the subject of religious freedom. "Congress shall make no law respecting an establishment of religion, or prohibiting the free exercise thereof; or abridging the freedom of speech, or of the press; or the right of the people peaceably to assemble, and to petition the government for a redress of grievances."

But as public education has damaged the ability of people to think rationally, and media has continued its assault on Christianity, freedom of religious expression has been incorrectly redefined as "freedom of worship." It is vital we understand the critical difference between these two. *Freedom of worship* is code for "gather in your churches and say and believe what you want, but don't you dare express it publicly." In other words, Christians are being bullied and intimidated to not share the gospel and the truth of God's Word in public, relegating us to a "holy huddle" within the walls of our church – the opposite of what Jesus commanded in Matthew 28:19-20.

How successful has the indoctrination by public education and media been in undermining the freedom of religious expression for our citizens? A 2016 poll conducted by Rasmussen Reports shows that only 29 percent of Americans support religious freedom laws protecting the religious conscience of business owners and individuals, while 64 percent disapprove. In other words, almost two-thirds of Americans oppose the first freedom guaranteed in the U.S. Constitution. Public education, combined with a corrupt, godless agenda-driven media, and fueled by the most powerful lobbying group in our history – the LGBTQ movement – have successfully convinced a strong majority of Americans that religious freedom of expression is limited to the confines of the four walls of the local church. Christians should be seen but not heard.

The result of step 4 is that Christians are warned that our deeply held religious beliefs and convictions had better be confined to the four walls of our church. Believe what you want, but don't you dare try to convince others you are right or accuse them of something as egregious as sinning against the God you believe in. But if you believe Satan and his minions will be satisfied and will stop their assault by silencing us publicly, you underestimate what is really happening.

Step 5: Implement full-blown persecution because of the "danger" of Biblical Christianity to society

Behind all the tolerance portrayed by liberals is an agenda to dismantle Christianity in America because the Bible firmly speaks against the immoral behaviors and values of the current liberal movement. Liberals believe the end justifies the means, and they will stop at nothing to implement a godless society where self-worship is the new standard of morality. In other words, if they believe their cause is a just one, even unjust or vicious attacks on those who oppose the movement are justified for the good of society. Adolph Hitler and Joseph Stalin believed the very same thing, and these evil men understood one very important point: Biblical Christianity was the major impediment to implementation of their agenda. Radical liberals understand this also.

When the LGBTQ began its concentrated push to legalize homosexual marriage, we were told they had no intention of forcing their beliefs on anyone who disagreed with them. But in the first few years since homosexual marriage was legalized, we have seen liberals act like sharks who can smell blood. Suddenly, gender dysphoria was the next great battleground, and a full-court press to allow people to change their gender began. Supported by some corrupt medical associations who saw tremendous potential for increased profit by supporting hormonal therapies and even radical gender-reconstruction surgeries, the transgender movement has rapidly gathered strong public support among Americans. This is in spite of the same medical community acknowledging there is no way the gender of a person can truly change and all that can be done is to accommodate their emotions by helping their bodies be conformed to their feelings.

Just a handful of years ago the subject of gender confusion was not even on the radar screen. Now a recent poll (Fusion Millennial) says that 50 percent of millennials believe gender is a "spectrum" not restricted to male or female and can be changed. Welcome to the next – and potentially determinative – battle against Biblical Christianity in America, one of which I am well aware and directly involved in.

Forcing Secular Humanism on Churches and Ministries

Our Christian radio station is located in De Pere, Wisconsin, a city directly adjacent to Green Bay. In the fall of 2017 the De Pere city council published its intent to consider, and ultimately pass, a non-discrimination ordinance giving self-identified transgenders complete protection and access to services provided by any organization within the city. Unlike some similar ordinances passed around the nation, De Pere's ordinance provided no exemption for religious churches and organizations. Despite a letter from our ministry leadership, along with five churches in De Pere that stated if a religious exemption was not added to the ordinance we would be forced to challenge its legality in court, the city council passed the ordinance with no alteration. Our ministry and those five churches, aided by the Pacific Justice Institute, have subsequently filed for an injunction to force the ordinance to include a strong religious exemption or be ruled unconstitutional.

By God's grace, the five churches and our ministry were granted victory in our lawsuit, with the judge striking down DePere's ordinance. But it is just a matter of time until courts decide to grant government increased power and control over what churches and religious organizations can and cannot do. So while we praise God for this initial victory, we prepare for the day when government is allowed to control what churches teach, who they hire, and the services they can provide.

We are grateful for the five solid Biblical churches in De Pere standing up to this discrimination and oppression. But as usual, I have witnessed a couple church leaders in our city cower under the guise of "love," not wanting to be seen as judgmental. When I shared the details of what the city of De Pere was passing into law, they stated this wasn't their battle. Is there any doubt these leaders will capitulate to anything the government mandates for the sake of their precious tax-exempt status and their desire to be the next megachurch? These cowardly pastors say the exact opposite of what Peter boldly stated in Acts 5:29. They are saying, "We must obey men rather than God!"

At the crux of the issue is the definition of a "place of public accommodation." Historically, courts have ruled that churches and religious organizations are *private* organizations and not places of public accommodation. The city of De Pere continued to insist that our ministry and local churches are considered places of public accommodation. Had they receive a favorable ruling, here are some of the potential consequences of their ordinance:

- Churches and ministries cannot refuse to hire homosexual or transgender applicants.

- We must allow them to use the bathroom facility they feel best coincides with whatever gender they are feeling that day. (Understand the LGBTQ movement believes a person's gender can vary from day to day based on how they feel on any given day.)

- LGBTQ organizers would be allowed to use Christian churches and ministries for public meetings and presentations. This would de facto lead people to believe that we support their godless agenda, bringing more confusion into the Christian community.

- We would be forced to supply any service offered to any other person (free radio airtime on our radio station and wedding ceremonies for churches) even if their beliefs and values contradicted God's Word. The LGBTQ movement would now have free access to promote their beliefs and events to our Christian audience, and we could say or do nothing to discourage people from participating.

While we were granted victory in our legal challenge, the swift change in public opinion, combined with increased judicial activism in many courts, lead to the logical conclusion that one day soon a court will rule to the contrary and, unless struck down firmly by the Supreme Court, churches in America will be forced to provide services like weddings to transgenders and homosexuals or lose their tax-exempt status and be subject to fines. Our Christian radio station would be forced to decide to either promote LGBTQ activities and their agenda or be shut down. And make no mistake, beyond being forced to comply with providing all services to people directly opposed to God, if a church or a ministry even addresses these issues as "sin" they will be threatened with hate-speech crimes and will be fined or eventually shut down. Our board of directors has already unanimously decided we will obey God rather than man even if it means time spent in jail. Churches and non-profit religious organizations will be forced to make one of two choices:

- They can maintain their tax-exempt advantage by complying with the government's insistence that speaking out against almost any sin identified in the Bible is hate speech and a danger to the good of society.

- They can choose to lose their tax-advantage status, affecting their financial viability, and be treated as for-profit businesses. But the rub there is that even for-profit businesses will be subject to hate-speech enforcement, being threatened with shutdown if they say or do anything deemed offensive to anyone else.

It does not take a rocket scientist to accurately predict that this threat to churches is not a matter of *if*, but *when*. And actually, it might be the best thing that could happen to professing Christians and churches: to be forced to decide once and for all if God or man will be obeyed (Acts 5:29). Once and for all, the confusion between Biblical and American

Christianity churches will be clearly defined. Then each professing Christian can choose which to belong to in choosing to worship God or self.

When laws like this are confirmed by the courts as constitutional and churches and religious organizations are viewed as places of public accommodation, the full financial and legal hammer of the government will come down on Biblical Christianity in America. Churches faithful to God's Word will be stripped of their tax-exempt status and eventually be driven underground, while American Christianity will be protected by a corrupt antichrist system that follows Satan rather than God.

Summary

- Creating doubt about truth

- Softening the church's resistance to this world by preaching unity and tolerance for anything

- Mocking, intimidating, and threatening Christians into silence and acceptance of their agenda

- Restricting the church to its four walls and eliminating its influence on society

- All-out persecution where Christians are identified as a serious threat to society

Where are we in America on this slide to apostasy in the professing church? The first three steps have clearly been accomplished by the enemy and he has all but accomplished step 4. We may only be a few short years away from witnessing real persecution coming to the Biblical church in America as his master plan comes to full fruition.

While none of us wishes to undergo real persecution, we are foolish to discount the strong probability of it knocking on our doors one day soon. True Christians should be seeking God in the midst of this coming storm, praying that when our loyalty and allegiance to God is tested, the Holy Spirit will give us the courage to stand firm for God and His Word.

> *For what does it profit a man if he gains the whole world and*
> *loses or forfeits himself? For whoever is ashamed of me and*
> *of my words, of him will the Son of Man be ashamed when*
> *he comes in his glory and the glory of the Father and of the*
> *holy angels.* (Luke 9:25-26)

Is your church leadership ashamed of Jesus or the words He spoke? Are you? Is your church leadership cowering behind deceptions like "Well, there are several ways we can interpret certain Scriptures"? Are you? Do you want Jesus to be ashamed of you when He returns in glory? Does that even remotely bother you? If it doesn't, your alleged faith in Him is certainly open to scrutiny and question.

American Christianity is not a form of Christianity that simply has a couple things wrong in its doctrines. It is representative of Babylon itself. It stands for everything Babylon treasured: self-worship, power, pride, and arrogance before a righteous and just God. It is the latest attempt of fallen, sinful man to somehow place himself on the same plane as God, or even unseat Him from His throne. And the price you will pay for your allegiance to man or self instead of God is an eternal, horrible one.

In Romans 1 the apostle Paul tells us what happens when men reject the truth about God:

> *And since they did not see fit to acknowledge God, God gave*
> *them up to a debased mind to do what ought not to be done.*
> *They were filled with all manner of unrighteousness, evil,*
> *covetousness, malice. They are full of envy, murder, strife,*
> *deceit, maliciousness. They are gossips, slanderers, haters of*
> *God, insolent, haughty, boastful, inventors of evil, disobedi-*
> *ent to parents, foolish, faithless, heartless, ruthless. Though*
> *they know God's righteous decree that those who practice*
> *such things deserve to die, they not only do them but give*
> *approval to those who practice them.* (Romans 1:28-32)

Your church may not be there yet, but if leaders continue to teach the doctrines of man as if they are from God, giving in to the ways of the world for the sake of growth, compromising on the gospel in insisting that "God will meet you halfway," compromising with secular culture instead of opposing it, and valuing unity over truth, it is only a matter of time. And if you are not equipped to spot deception cleverly disguised as truth, and you stand before God condemned, the argument of "But my pastor taught me the wrong things" will be rejected by God. The Germans who carried out the murder of millions of Jews during the Holocaust made the argument that they were only following orders. Their argument was rejected out of hand. Likewise, our arguments of ignorance or "just following orders" will condemn us for eternity when we stand before Jesus Christ as judge of all mankind.

So the problem is clear. We have a professing Christian church that is eliminating the doctrines and principles of God's Word, replacing them with a religion of secular humanism where morality is defined by sinful man instead of a righteous God. A church that is teaching the traditions of man as if they were from God, just like the first-century Pharisees. A church in transition from a house of prayer to a *den of robbers* (Matthew 21:13). A church that is preaching a gospel contrary to the one taught in the Bible.

So what do we do about this abomination unfolding right before our eyes? In 1517 a man named Martin Luther faced a very similar problem. He started what would become known as the Protestant Reformation by publishing his Ninety-Five Theses, putting Roman Catholicism on notice that things needed to change. The Protestant Reformation was arguably the single-most influential moment of Christianity since the life of Jesus Christ and the expansion of the early church. But as is usually the case, even those who fight corruption are eventually corrupted themselves. Today, many Protestant and evangelical churches are returning to the vomit of biblical apostasy. And in the zeal for a unity that contradicts the Bible and actually will be used to build the false one-world religion of the final days, churches of almost every denomination along with the Catholic Church are marching swiftly to Babylon itself in the latest effort to topple God and take its place on His throne.

Perhaps it is time for a "Second Reformation" – one that will clearly delineate itself from the journey to Babylon taking over American Christianity. One that will clearly contrast with what American

Christianity has become. A contrast so unmistakably clear and obvious that every professing Christian can once and for all decide the path he wants to follow and the church he wants to hitch his wagon to.

Chapter Five

History Repeating Itself

The Protestant Reformation was the result of several concerns shared by Martin Luther and others about the theology and structure of Roman Catholicism. Among the theological concerns were the selling of indulgences to help dead relatives escape purgatory, the elevation of Mary far beyond her biblical scope, the authority of the popes, and Catholic teachings that held church traditions on a par with, or even above the Bible. But another factor rarely discussed was Luther's concern that the Roman Catholic Church had become so intertwined with worldly governments that the two were almost inseparable.

There can be little doubt of the positive effects of this Reformation, but as Proverbs 26:11 says, a fool who repeats his folly is like a dog returning to its vomit. And slowly over the centuries, as the Protestant Reformation led to the establishment of thousands of Christian denominations, the professing church has become theologically splintered. "Doctrinal distinctives" became sources of contention, and in our argument over these distinctives we lose sight of the big picture happening around us. We major in the minors, taking our eyes off what the enemy is doing to subvert true Christianity. We fight over relatively minor differences, all while the enemy is working to sow discord, undermining the fundamental biblical doctrines of Christianity.

Here are three major points of the Reformation and how they are resurfacing under American Christianity:

- The infallibility of the pope and church leaders

- Elevating human doctrine and tradition to the level of Scripture

- The intertwining of the church with human government

Each of these is resurfacing rapidly but subtly in American Christianity, leading unsuspecting Christians into a religious system that resembles Babylon more than Biblical Christianity.

Infallibility of Church Leadership

While there is no one official source of infallibility in American Christianity, make no mistake that behind the scenes there is a growing attitude that church leadership should never be questioned or corrected when their theology drifts from biblical truth. When some of the prosperity preachers are challenged about their false teachings and massive accumulation of wealth on the backs of ignorant followers, you will hear the Scriptures twisted to warn not to touch "God's anointed." This is simply spiritual bullying made possible by our ignorance of God's Word as we increasingly trust anyone who claims to be a pastor or teacher, along with our growing obsession with the things of this world.

When I began publicly speaking out over the concerns I saw with Willow Creek Church, I was confronted by three pastors who accused me of dividing and undermining the church. But as the conversation unfolded, the real agenda of these pastors came to light. They accused me of causing extra work for them because now "church members were asking me questions about what I preached or the vision of the church." Then came the spiritual bullying. One of them asked me sarcastically, "So where did you get your theological training from? What Bible college did you attend?" I answered that my knowledge came from a passion for reading the Bible, sitting under a group of mature Christians who mentored me for years as I grew, and realizing the only thing qualified to correctly interpret the Bible was the Bible itself.

I then turned the tables on him and asked where he received his theological training. When he proudly answered, "Fuller Theological Seminary," I promised I would not hold that against him, given Fuller's recent slide into spiritual confusion by accepting unrepentant sinners like homosexuals to lead and teach, and Fuller's professors questioning the Bible's authenticity and accuracy.

I then respectfully asked all three of them if I could ask them a couple questions regarding their spiritual doctrines. After one question – what is the nature and character of God and is it eternal or subject to change – they left because they said I had no standing to question them as pastors. It is that arrogance permeating American Christianity that is as dangerous as anything within it: the hubris of thinking only pastors can rightly interpret and teach the Word of God. Understand that to American Christian pastors and leaders, you are to blindly follow and never question them. Their outward appearance of confidence is but a shell masquerading insecurity and a conscience that knows they are wrong. And if we dare question them, they will become very defensive and pull rank on you just like the Pharisees of the first century and the Roman Catholic leadership of Luther's time. We owe it to them to point out their contradictions and then pray that the Holy Spirit opens their eyes to the deception that is blinding them.

I have talked with so many frustrated Christians who have serious concerns about the doctrines being taught or the direction of their church, only to be dismissed or spiritually bullied when they had the courage to respectfully question their church leaders. I believe this is a direct result of the obsession of the Church Growth Movement modeled by Peter Drucker to Rick Warren and Bill Hybels, along with the obsession over Warren's Purpose Driven Church model. We showed earlier how Warren's model suggests opposing and humiliating church members who dare to question the church's vision.

Hand in hand with the growing arrogance of the leaders of American Christianity is the spiritual malpractice carried out upon husbands in the church. There is a thought process within the leaders, perhaps unconscious, that the last thing they want is men who understand God's Word, because they could spot errors in doctrine or the direction of church leadership. So they are not taught how to become true spiritual leaders out of fear that they might actually start to lead within the church and even in their own families.

As radical feminism infiltrates our society and subsequently American Christianity, could pastors be ignoring teaching men how to be spiritual leaders in the church and their own homes because they secretly enjoy being admired and looked up to by the wives of these men? I realize this is a serious subject, and I do not believe the vast majority of these pastors intend for that to happen. But as spiritual leaders, who are subject to human pride like all of us, receive compliments and praise for their work and leadership, perhaps unconsciously they crave even more flattery and attention. Whether it's a conscious effort of subverting husbands or not, Paul points this out:

> *For God is not a God of confusion but of peace. As in all the churches of the saints, the women should keep silent in the churches. For they are not permitted to speak, but should be in submission, as the Law also says. If there is anything they desire to learn, let them ask their husbands at home. For it is shameful for a woman to speak in church. Or was it from you that the word of God came? Or are you the only ones it has reached? If anyone thinks that he is a prophet, or spiritual, he should acknowledge that the things I am writing to you are a command of the Lord.* (1 Corinthians 14:33-37)

In light of the radical feminist movement taking over secular culture and subsequently infiltrating American Christianity, anyone who teaches these Scriptures will be accused of being a chauvinist. But this is the Word of God! Are we to simply throw it aside or ignore it because it makes us feel uncomfortable or might meet with the world's criticism and scorn? The sad answer from those immersed in the church growth or seeker-friendly movements would be yes, because they have bought the lie that the schemes of man, instead of God, grow the church.

Let's be clear. Nowhere does the Bible teach or infer that men are superior and women inferior in God's eyes. But let us be equally clear that God has established an order for church and family, and men are ordained as the leaders of these two crucial institutions. But instead of trusting God and His Word, American Christianity panders to and adopts the ways of secular society to appear loving and tolerant. Truth is often uncomfortable and inconvenient. But God's Word from Genesis

1 to Revelation 22 is eternal truth, and to discount or even change it for personal convenience, or to be seen as loving and accepting to a sinful world, is spiritual malpractice.

So while church leadership may put on a façade by publicly stating their imperfection in interpreting and applying God's Word, make no mistake, there is an underlying and growing movement to go back to pre-Reformation times where whatever church leaders say and believe is beyond reproach. The members of the church are to follow blindly and never touch God's anointed. And if you dare question or challenge American Christianity church leaders about the doctrines being taught or the direction and vision of the church, you will be labeled a Sanballat.

Elevating Human and Church Tradition to the Level of Scripture

The evidence of this is seen in the growing number of denominations and churches in American Christianity distorting the teachings of the Bible to accommodate secular society, and professing Christians who love this world more than God. God's Word is being diminished to a series of stories with varying mixtures of truth and fable. The biblical creation account, the garden of Eden, and the global flood have become matters of speculation rather than biblical truth. The Old Testament is ignored or even distorted because either pastors cannot accurately reconcile God's words and actions in the Old Testament with Jesus' words in the New Testament, or the Old Testament narrative is inconsistent with the message the church wants to deliver to members and the secular world.

Secular culture continues to infiltrate the church as it is invited in with open arms, changing the culture and leadership model of the church, and leading to a watering down or outright distortion of God's Word to accommodate that sinful culture. And because Christians are unconsciously being trained to ignore studying God's Word and trust in church leadership instead, most professing Christians don't realize they are on a fast track toward Babylon. When you stand before God and are found guilty, don't look to your pastor or favorite televangelist to save you, because he'll have his own problems, as teachers are held to a higher standard by God.

As an increasingly sinful culture infiltrates American Christianity, we see doctrines being distorted or changed and the church accommodating the culture in not only what is taught but also in how church is conducted. To accommodate the hubris and self-righteousness of people, sin is discounted and replaced with a "best life now" philosophy that focuses on the benefits of salvation without the responsibilities. Church worship teams have become the focus of many churches in order to properly entertain people who will settle for nothing less, at the expense of a deep, thorough sermon which they will only find boring anyway, taking away precious time they could be at home sleeping or watching sports.

Church youth groups have become a gathering for fun and games with little preparation for young people to defend against the attacks of a world where now up to 80 percent of professing Christian youth leave the faith once they go off to college. Our youth have serious, important questions about God and life, but we squander the opportunity to teach them because we probably fear they might ask something we lack a biblical answer for. Parents increasingly shove the responsibility to teach their children about God off on youth pastors who might know little more than their children, or who themselves have bought into the secular culture.

Genuine moves of the Holy Spirit in churches where sinners are convicted of their sins and people have their eyes opened to the amazing truth and grace of God, are being replaced by superficial spiritual moves carefully orchestrated by just the right song or manipulative message from the pulpit. In some churches people literally bark like dogs or cluck like chickens, thinking this is how God operates. There is no genuine conviction of the Holy Spirit leading to tears of repentance; rather, there's a carefully orchestrated move of a false spirit or our flesh that makes God's church look more like a traveling circus instead of holy ground with the presence of God's Spirit.

Here is a question that will help you determine the condition of your heart and the spiritual condition of your church: When you wake up on Sunday morning and realize you will shortly head to church, what is your initial emotion and thought? One of obligation and inconvenience like going to your job? Or one of great joy and expectation that you get to hear God's Word and experience meaningful worship and fellowship?

Now a second question: How do you feel and what do you think about when you are leaving church? Are you relieved that your "duty" to attend is over for another week? Or is there even a remote sense of regret that your time of fellowship is coming to an end? Did the sermon have a profound impact in thinking about the life you lead, making a truthful self-assessment as to whether you are walking closer to or being drawn further away from God and the life that is mandated upon the true born-again believer?

As American Christianity is transformed more into the image of secular culture in what is taught and how church is conducted, we become numb to what the world is committed to doing to us: Drawing us away from God. And when we drift far enough, we can no longer recognize Biblical Christianity from American Christianity. We will find we are right where this world wants us to be, because we are ripe for a deception so cunning that the vast majority of professing Christian churches in America will welcome a radical change that will seal their fate and the fate of their members as enemies of God.

The Intertwining of Church and Government into an Unholy Alliance against God

Look at this like a geyser bubbling under the surface, occasionally spewing out small amounts of hot water. It may look harmless or even beautiful on the surface, but it is an indication of seismic activity that is a catastrophe waiting to happen. One day it explodes and creates havoc and destruction.

Starting with the Johnson Amendment in 1954, churches have slowly but systematically been bullied into silence so their non-tax status would not be threatened. Spiritual issues like abortion, sexuality, and gender are being presented as political issues and off-limits within the church so that they do not cause division. The chess pieces are being manipulated by Satan for American Christianity to repeat the mistake of Catholic and Protestant churches as Hitler rose to power: Cooperate with government for the good of the people and society or face the consequences of an oppressive government.

As churches soften their stances on abortion, homosexuality, and gender confusion, and courts continue to restrict what Christians can do or even say in public, the stage is being set for another holocaust, but this time it will be Biblical Christians who will bear the wrath of a world that hates God. And American Christianity will ally with government in its silencing by any means necessary anyone who stands on the truth of the Bible. Remember these words of Jesus?

> "But be on your guard. For they will deliver you over to councils, and you will be beaten in synagogues, and you will stand before governors and kings for my sake, to bear witness before them. And the gospel must first be proclaimed to all nations. And when they bring you to trial and deliver you over, do not be anxious beforehand what you are to say, but say whatever is given you in that hour, for it is not you who speak, but the Holy Spirit. And brother will deliver brother over to death, and the father his child, and children will rise against parents and have them put to death. And you will be hated by all for my name's sake. But the one who endures to the end will be saved." (Mark 13:9-13)

This will happen one day, perhaps much sooner than we expect. American Christianity itself, bowing to the ways of this world instead of God, will turn on true believers who are seen as a threat to their power and influence, and will assist the world in silencing and persecuting true believers.

We are getting glimpses into the tactics that Satan's minions will use to discredit and even destroy anyone who opposes his agenda. They tried to destroy Jack Phillips, the Colorado cake baker who refused to design a cake for a homosexual wedding ceremony. They have tried to destroy any Christian businessperson who refuses to compromise with the sin of this world. And most recently, they have sunk to new lows in the tactics they use to destroy anyone who is seen as a threat to their beliefs and values.

"I" Am Brett Kavanaugh

We are witnessing an intentional movement to dismantle freedom of speech and religious expression in our nation because the evil hearts of fallen men and women, turned over to a reprobate mind by God because they have rejected the truth about Him (Romans 1), value the murder of innocent children in the womb more than anything. Liberals who cry out against the death penalty for fear a single person might unjustly die are hell-bent on making sure millions of innocent children are given a death sentence every year without due process. And this constitutional protection of due process, the belief that a person is innocent until proven guilty beyond a reasonable doubt, is under attack by liberals who claim to be fair, reasonable, and tolerant but are the exact opposite of what they claim. They will do anything they deem necessary to destroy anyone who opposes their atheist, Marxist worldview. There is no due process with these people because that requires logic, reasonableness, and evidence. As a Bible-believing Christian or conservative in this nation, you are guilty of being a homophobe, misogynist, or racist despite the evidence presented by your life.

Satan is a master at taking something that initially looks good and twisting it into something destructive and evil. We are witnessing his latest tactic in the Me Too movement. Women around the nation are coming forward to share their stories of how they claim they have been sexually harassed and intimidated by men in power. And I have no doubt that many of these stories are credible, and we should be glad that men are being put on notice that using power or authority to manipulate women sexually should never be tolerated. So on the surface the Me Too movement can be a very good thing. But, consistent with his historic tactics, Satan distorts something good by just tweaking it a little bit with a lie. And the lie we hear repeated over and over by the radical feminists Satan is using is this: "Women never lie about these things."

Because of the rise in radical feminism, fueled by Satan's desire to undermine God's perfect order, any man who is accused of abusing his authority for sexual gain is guilty the day the accusation is made, with no real chance to prove his innocence. Due process has been completely turned upside down. Instead of being considered innocent until proven guilty, men are now guilty until they can prove the accusations are 100-percent false, and even that might be insufficient! Understand that this systematic effort to dismantle due process goes far beyond the Me Too movement. It is at the heart of the radical, godless Marxist movement to replace God with government as the ruler of men. No longer is a citizen innocent until proven guilty by direct evidence; now a mere anonymous, discredited accusation with no evidence or corroboration can be used to destroy anyone who stands in the way of Satan's agenda, supported by an evil world system. Me Too is simply Satan's latest tool to create chaos that will call for order: a new world order where a select few, led by Antichrist, will give Satan what he has always desired – to be worshiped as god.

Judge Brett Kavanaugh, who by the accounts of hundreds of friends, co-workers, and fellow professionals is a man of highest moral character and eminently qualified to sit on the Supreme Court, was a target of hatred, lies, and personal destruction by evil so forceful that only Satan could be its mastermind. We will not take the time to critique the hearts of career democrat politicians who joyfully set out to destroy Judge Kavanaugh, because their history indicates they are capable of nothing else but the politics of personal destruction. We will again turn our focus to how American Christianity itself was a willing co-conspirator in this evil. But first a word of caution about how technology will play a huge role in the plans of a world worshiping Antichrist.

Artificial Intelligence is all the rage of the scientific and technology industries these days. Technology, presented as a servant of mankind, may one day soon rise to the level of master over it. Today China has more than three hundred million cameras that can monitor every move or conversation of its citizens. Smartphones can be used to spy on users and provide patterns of purchases, conversations, and personal interests that build algorithms which will be used to manipulate and control users.

When you apply for a mortgage or a credit card, rent an apartment, or even apply for a job, your credit score is used to assess your level of personal responsibility and character. China has officially announced a new credit scoring system called the "Social Credit System" that not only monitors promptness in paying your bills, but also uses information obtained through its comprehensive spy network monitored by three hundred million public cameras, information obtained from individual smart devices and social media, and allegiance or verbal resistance to the communist regime, to determine if you are worthy of employment or credit. Does this sound even remotely familiar to you as a Christian? If not, you might well be immersed in a church of American Christianity that dismisses Bible prophecy. This sounds remarkably like the "mark of the beast" we are warned about in Revelation:

> *And it was allowed to give breath to the image of the beast, so that the image of the beast might even speak and might cause those who would not worship the image of the beast to be slain. Also it causes all, both small and great, both rich and poor, both free and slave, to be marked on the right hand or the forehead, so that no one can buy or sell unless he has the mark, that is, the name of the beast or the number of its name.* (Revelation 13:15-17)

As our younger people, enamored by and completely embracing new technology, are increasingly convinced that socialism, which is just a precursor to godless communism, is a good thing, our nation is on the verge of becoming a totalitarian state like China, where government is worshiped and God is eliminated. As these younger people become more and more influential in American Christianity, which already cowers at fear of the world, American Christianity will soon become a component of Antichrist's false prophet doing his will.

> *For certain people have crept in unnoticed who long ago were designated for this condemnation, ungodly people, who pervert the grace of our God into sensuality and deny our only Master and Lord, Jesus Christ.* (Jude 1:4)

The democrat who was the head attack dog against Judge Kavanaugh was Senator Cory Booker, a professing Christian and the very man Bill Hybels and Willow Creek Church held up in highest esteem at their Global Leadership Summit as a leader Christians should emulate. This deceptive liberal politician, who was heralded as a great leader in the greatest of American Christianity churches, did everything he could to destroy a man of character and integrity. And if you think for one minute this is not the beginning of persecution of true Christians in America, then you are under a great deception by the enemy.

Here is something that is crucial for committed Biblical Christians to understand: *You and I are the enemies of American Christianity.* Make no mistake, consciously or unconsciously, the leaders of American Christianity see us as Sanballats standing in the way of their personal prosperity and reputation to a world that hates God. Whether your church has sold out to prosperity preaching or the seeker-friendly or purpose-driven movements, you and I stand in the way of their agenda of power. They are poised to do exactly what the Catholic and Protestant churches did as Hitler rose to power: bow to him instead of God so they can maintain protection from a human government instead of trusting God, all for the sake of money, power, and reputation. And here is the really sad thing: many of them are not conscious of what they are doing and will actually think they are serving God by turning on you and me.

> *"I have said all these things to you to keep you from falling away. They will put you out of the synagogues. Indeed, the hour is coming when whoever kills you will think he is offering service to God. And they will do these things because they have not known the Father, nor me. But I have said these things to you, that when their hour comes you may remember that I told them to you."* (John 16:1-4)

The unholy alliance of oppressive self-worshiping government and secular culture and American Christianity will stop at nothing to silence anyone standing in the way of their agenda.

Look carefully at what Judge Kavanaugh was put through: Attacks on his family, his personal character, and his career by liars who ignored evidence, common sense, and decency because he dares to think that abortion (murder) is not morally right. Understand he never even hinted he would ever vote to overturn *Roe v. Wade.* In fact, he testified that Supreme Court precedence must always be held in the highest regard by succeeding courts! But even the slightest fear that he might restrict in any way the murder of millions of innocent children every year sent liberals and phony Christians into a lather of hatred and viciousness never seen in our nation before.

Now imagine you or I as committed disciples of Jesus sitting in a similar chair, and the abuse of the power of technology is added to their arsenal of hate and deception! If you are deemed an enemy of society because of your views on gender, sexuality, or abortion, and your church is threatened with scrutiny because you attend there, do you think for one minute they will defend and protect you given all they would be risking? You will be offered as a sacrifice to their god in a heartbeat, and they will justify their actions believing they are serving God! Because of the growing unholy alliance between a corrupt government and a fake Christianity, just like the pre-Reformation days, the day is coming soon when anyone who stands against this antichrist alliance will be subject to what Judge Kavanaugh experienced and more. When we forget or dismiss history, we are doomed to repeat it.

> *And I saw, coming out of the mouth of the dragon and out of the mouth of the beast and out of the mouth of the false prophet, three unclean spirits like frogs. For they are demonic spirits, performing signs, who go abroad to the kings of the whole world, to assemble them for battle on the great day of God the Almighty.* (Revelation 16:13-14)

> *Then one of the seven angels who had the seven bowls came and said to me, "Come, I will show you the judgment of the great prostitute who is seated on many waters, with whom the kings of the earth have committed sexual immorality, and with the wine of whose sexual immorality the dwellers on earth have become drunk." And he carried me away in the Spirit into a wilderness, and I saw a woman sitting on a scarlet beast that was full of blasphemous names, and it had seven heads and ten horns. The woman was arrayed in purple and scarlet, and adorned with gold and jewels and pearls, holding in her hand a golden cup full of abominations and the impurities of her sexual immorality. And on her forehead was written a name of mystery: "Babylon the*

great, mother of prostitutes and of earth's abominations."
And I saw the woman, drunk with the blood of the saints,
the blood of the martyrs of Jesus. When I saw her, I mar-
veled greatly. (Revelation 17:1-6)

Do not fall for the belief that the woman on the beast is represented only by the Catholic Papacy. While its part is prominent, American Christianity, the prevailing religion in the world's most powerful nation, will play a very prominent role in the rise of spiritual Babylon that will support Antichrist as his spiritual mouthpiece. And like Judge Kavanaugh, we who choose to obey God instead of men will one day sit in the seat of hatred, lies, and outright evil that Kavanaugh just sat in. And the weapons of the enemy will be greatly enhanced by a technology that is capable of deception so great that it can quote you on something you never said or would say. With legal due process being destroyed before our eyes, you will be found guilty of crimes against society because of your beliefs, regardless of the life you lead or what you truly believe. You are simply in the way of the path of a world which is pledging allegiance to Satan and you will be destroyed. And if you look to your American Christian church for moral or spiritual support, you will be turned over to the enemy and your church will actually think it is serving God! And it is, but not the God of the Bible; rather, the god of this world, Satan himself.

I am Judge Kavanaugh. And so are you if you remain faithful to God in the coming years. Is all this worth it to you? If not, you are not fit to follow Jesus. These are His words, not mine:

"Do not think that I have come to bring peace to the earth. I
have not come to bring peace, but a sword. For I have come
to set a man against his father, and a daughter against her
mother, and a daughter-in-law against her mother-in-law.
And a person's enemies will be those of his own household.
Whoever loves father or mother more than me is not worthy
of me, and whoever loves son or daughter more than me is
not worthy of me. And whoever does not take his cross and
follow me is not worthy of me. Whoever finds his life will

lose it, and whoever loses his life for my sake will find it." (Matthew 10:34-39)

Satan is older than us and he has honed his craft as the father of lies over thousands of years of experience with sinful man. He keeps using the same tactics because they work. He has successfully infiltrated American Christianity just as he did the early Roman Catholic Church that Luther stood against. American Christianity is repeating the same mistakes Roman Catholicism stood guilty of in Luther's time:

- The infallibility of self-proclaimed church leadership

- Elevating human doctrine and tradition to the level of Scripture

- The intertwining of the church with evil human government

The choice is becoming crystal clear for anyone who professes to be a Christian: We either go along with it to get along with others and support this unholy alliance of government and religion, or we become like the men of Issachar in 1 Chronicles 12:32 who understood the times and what God's people needed to get done.

Chapter Six

A Christian Reformation for Such a Time as This

L uther did not intend to dismantle the Catholic Church. He loved it but understood the need to seriously reform it as it strayed from the truth of God's Word.

We love the church in America and do not want to see it dismantled either. But every bit as much as in the time of Luther, a radical reformation based solely on the Word of God is necessary. Just as in Luther's time, the souls of millions unknowingly being led into Babylon are at stake. And we are reaching a crucial point in time. If American Christianity continues on its current trajectory for a decade or so, she will eventually align with Antichrist in opposition to God. And God's Word says anyone who pledges allegiance to Antichrist is beyond salvation. They will be condemned to eternal hell.

It is out of sincere love and concern for pastors and the people God has given them to lead that I outline what I think this reformation needs to address. We must understand that the vast majority of pastors and church leadership being seduced by American Christianity are unaware of what is happening to them. They are people who genuinely love God and are trying to do what they believe is right. But when we rely on our human understanding to battle an enemy as strong as Satan, we are no match for him. He is the father of lies and the prince of this world, and we in our human strength and wisdom are no match whatsoever against him. Only God's Word and Spirit can crush him.

Stop Misrepresenting God and His Word

Stop treating the Word of God with less reverence than God demands. God exalts His name and Word *above all things* (Psalm 138:2). Start doing the same. The Bible is the inspired, eternally true Word of God which never changes. It is the only source of truth, period.

Stop suggesting that somehow God has abandoned His eternal righteous and just nature to compromise in reaching out to save sinful man. The God of the Old Testament is the same as the God of the New Testament. His nature and character never change and He never compromises. The Bible can only be correctly interpreted and understood when we solely use the Bible to interpret itself. And when we try to interpret the Bible from a faulty starting point of not understanding the nature and character of God, there is no way we can accurately interpret or teach it.

Please start teaching the Bible with complete accuracy and context. For example, the book of Malachi has been reduced to a single verse in American Christianity – Malachi 3:10, which is being used to manipulate Christians to give to the church and to prosperity ministries. But the book of Malachi's overriding message is God's displeasure and anger over a corrupt priesthood and a people whose worship had become heartless. Be intellectually honest about God's Word and stop cherry-picking verses that serve your human agenda.

Please stop ignoring the Old Testament as if you either do not understand it or are ashamed of God's words and actions in it. Be able to answer Christians with legitimate questions or confusion about God's Word:

- How do we correctly reconcile the law with grace? Why are we commanded to still keep parts of the law but not others? What did Jesus mean when He said He came not to abolish the law but to fulfill it?

- How can a loving God order the complete destruction of people in Sodom and Gomorrah and Jericho and still be loving and merciful? Why did Moses command the people to stone adulterers while Jesus discouraged the religious leaders of His time from doing so?

- What is Paul saying when he deals with matters of conscience? Does this mean we can decide what is right or wrong for us personally?

- How can we live in this world, and be witnesses to lost souls, by speaking the truth with complete grace and love? What does it mean to be *in* the world but not *of* it? What does that look like according to the Bible?

The Gospel

Stop diminishing or adding to the one true gospel. The gospel is a holy, righteous, and just God reconciling sinful man to Himself. God does not compromise or meet us halfway. God detests all sin and man must be punished for his sin and disobedience. So the just and gracious God of the universe looked down on hopelessly lost and sinful man and sent His Son Jesus Christ, God in the flesh, to live as one of us, satisfying God's wrath against sin by dying for sinful man. Man is reconciled to God by confessing his sinful state, repenting of his sinful ways (a change of heart and mind that leads to increasingly righteous and holy living), and trusting solely in Jesus Christ as his Lord and Savior. The true born-again believer acknowledges that Jesus Christ is both our only savior and Lord of all things, including our lives, and our lives should reflect increasing holiness and obedience to God's Word.

Start Warning People about the Return of the Lord

Please start taking biblical prophecy seriously and start teaching it consistently. Challenge church members with Jesus' warning that many of them who think they are saved might not be (Matthew 7:22-23). It is fine to tell people how Jesus came to offer salvation for sinful man, but start teaching about His return as judge of all men and the consequences if we are not truly born again.

Jesus came the first time to offer sinful man forgiveness of sins and eternal life with God through His death, burial, and resurrection to all who believe and trust in Him alone. He will return again to judge all men with the Word He has spoken. Every human being will either spend eternity with God in heaven or be eternally condemned to life in hell separated from God. There are no second chances after death. Preach the return of the Lord with passion and urgency. The eternal souls of men are at stake, so please preach the entire truth and context of God's Word – the encouraging verses *and* those that admonish. People deserve the complete truth.

Stop Obeying Men Instead of God

Stop compromising with culture and secular government in order to be more acceptable in the eyes of a world that increasingly hates God. Stop worrying about being seeker friendly and let the gospel and the Word of God convict men of their sin and rebellion against God, warning of the consequences of failing to do so. Preach the whole counsel of God's Word with truth and grace instead of implying through omission that grace is a license for Christians to go on sinning and for the world to continue in its rebellion against God.

Please stop worrying about protecting your tax-exempt status when it is impeding you from boldly proclaiming truth. Stop all your ill-fated attempts at church growth by adopting the ways of man instead of obeying God. As in the book of Acts, preach the Word, pray, experience meaningful and scriptural Christian fellowship, and God will add to the numbers of those being saved. Stop trying to reinvent Christ's church by infusing human wisdom, which is foolishness to God.

Stop subtly preaching that "Jesus accepts you right where you are." Instead, preach the truth: Jesus does reach out to us in our sin and depravity but demands confession, repentance, and complete faith and trust in Him alone. He does reach out to us in our sinful depravity, but He then demands contrite hearts and heartfelt confession and repentance.

The Role and Responsibilities of Church Leadership

Please take the responsibilities of church leadership in the Bible seriously. The role of leaders in Biblical Christianity is as undershepherds, guiding the flock assigned to them by Jesus as head shepherd. The role of pastors and elders is to teach the Word as God intended it, equip the saints for good works of the Holy Spirit, share the gospel with lost sinners, and make committed disciples of Jesus Christ. Any other vision or purpose for the church is man-made.

Elders, stop burdening the pastor with responsibilities God does not ask of him in His Word. Make sure your pastor is paid sufficiently so as not to have his family burdened. When considering a new pastor, do not fall for what the Israelites did when desiring a king: looking at human qualities (Saul). Forget about personal charisma or speaking style, and prayerfully seek a man who loves God more than anything, knows and can correctly teach the Bible, and desires God's agenda, not man's.

Pastors, stop learning how to become better leaders and dedicate your efforts to learning God's Word in correct context and relying on the Holy Spirit to influence people and grow His church. Replace feel-good sermons with convicting sermons from God's Word that remind us of His holiness and His command that we pursue holiness through His Word and Spirit, grateful that we have been saved from the eternal punishment of our sins, and with a passion to pursue holy living.

In accordance with the Scriptures, the church should be teaching and equipping men to become strong, loving spiritual leaders of their wives and children. When the church fails to do this, they undermine God's order and purpose for husbands. Husbands are to teach the Word to their wives, answering any questions they have about God's Word.

Start teaching, encouraging, and challenging men in your church to become strong spiritual leaders of their wives and families. Teach them what it means to love their wives as Christ loves His church. Prayerfully identify strong but submissive Christian women and encourage them to teach younger women how to become Proverbs 31 wives, submitting to and honoring their husbands. Help women understand that while God values women equally to men, the responsibilities of a Christian wife are different from those of her husband.

Encourage the men you lead to ask any questions or express any concerns they might have over the direction or programs in the church.

Unity in the Body of Christ

Please stop facilitating a "human unity" built on the teachings and wisdom of man, where disagreements over crucial biblical doctrine are dismissed for the sake of everyone getting along, and focus instead on what Jesus wants the church to unify around: a pursuit of holiness by the conviction of His Word and Spirit. Teach what the Bible teaches about the identity of the church: repentant sinners saved by the grace of God, seeking to be sanctified as part of the eternal bride of Christ. Stop allowing unrepentant sinners to remain as members of the church. The Bible warns us this is a danger to them and to the church. Encourage spiritual transparency and accountability for church members in an environment that is not hostile to confessing our sins to one another, and where all members are safe to seek help against the sins we struggle with. Start to take the responsibility of church discipline seriously (Matthew 18; 1 Corinthians 5). Understand and implement the biblical doctrine that unrepentant sinners should be removed from the church for their benefit and the church's if they are confronted with their sin and refuse to repent.

Be Good Stewards of the Finances God Provides

Please stop the capital campaigns for a new, beautiful church that might attract unbelievers or new members who are impressed with the comforts of this world, and instead start supporting committed missionary work around the world and in our community. Place a greater emphasis on utilizing all God provides toward serious evangelism, discipleship, and meeting the physical needs of church members unable to provide for themselves.

Encourage church members to be generous with all God has provided for them in money and time, to not only provide for the local church but also anywhere else they believe God is leading them to support His work.

Make Biblical Apologetics a Top Priority in the Church

*Learn and teach the principles of correct
biblical interpretation so church leadership and
members can spot and refute deception*

Start taking seriously your responsibilities to teach church members how to spot clever deception that Satan masquerades as truth. Realize that you are not the only spiritual influence in the lives of your church members. You have them for an hour or two a week, while false prophets and teachers influence them around the clock through social media and money mongers masquerading as Christian ministries. We are in church an hour or two a week. We live in a world that hates God and wants to deceive us the remaining 166 hours a week. Help members to spot lies and deception and the world's subtle but effective methods of drawing us away from God.

Teach them how to interpret the Bible correctly by understanding God-given principles of causality, non-contradiction, and biblical conjunctives so they can discern truth from clever deception.

Teach your church members how the world is cleverly deceiving them through media, public education, and government. Equip them to know and share the gospel with family, friends, neighbors, and co-workers. Start equipping young people instead of placating or entertaining them in what you call "youth ministry."

*Stop forcing couples with marital issues or people suffering
from addiction or emotional issues to depend on humanist
psychology or counseling as their resource for help*

The church should be the primary resource for marital issues between husbands and wives and for Christians struggling with problems in this life. Please stop abandoning them to humanist counselors and psychologists who will do more damage than good and lead them further from God. Pastors, elders, and properly trained church members should be qualified biblical counselors to help church members address problems and concerns.

Stop trying to emulate the world to attract people to church.
In doing so you are becoming more like the world

Stop attracting people to church with ways and comforts of this world, because what you use to *attract* them will be necessary to *keep* them in your church. This can only lead to a polluting of the spiritual purity Jesus wants in His church. As the first-century church did, model our gatherings around serious study of God's Word, heartfelt prayer, a sharing of all God has given us with one another, and remembering the sacrifice of Jesus on the cross. Let God, not our human cunning or methods, add to the church those that are being saved.

Stop cowering from serious spiritual issues in society like abortion, sexuality, and gender because it may lead some people to leave your church. Stop fearing the world and its financial and social pressures that are trying to silence the church.

Start taking seriously God's warning to church
leadership as "watchmen on the wall"

> *"So you, son of man, I have made a watchman for the house of Israel. Whenever you hear a word from my mouth, you shall give them warning from me. If I say to the wicked, O wicked one, you shall surely die, and you do not speak to warn the wicked to turn from his way, that wicked person shall die in his iniquity, but his blood I will require at your hand. But if you warn the wicked to turn from his way, and he does not turn from his way, that person shall die in his iniquity, but you will have delivered your soul."* (Ezekiel 33:7-9)

> *"But whoever causes one of these little ones who believe in me to sin, it would be better for him to have a great millstone fastened around his neck and to be drowned in the depth of the sea."* (Matthew 18:6)

> *Obey your leaders and submit to them,* **for they are keeping watch over your souls, as those who will have to give an account.** *Let them do this with joy and not with groaning,*

for that would be of no advantage to you. (Hebrews 13:17, emphasis added)

If you believe you have been called by God to be a leader in the church, take these warnings seriously! God will hold you accountable for what is taught and the influence you have on believers under your watch. If you do not think you have been called by God to lead, then please get out of the way. Embrace the responsibilities of Christian leadership, not just the benefits.

Summary

While perhaps not an exhaustive list, these "Reformation" issues must be addressed in any church that is serious about being a Biblical Christian church that submits to God. Every one of us is capable of being deceived or distracted by the enemy and the prince of this world, and church leadership is no exception. But being deceived in itself is not a serious crime. However, doubling down on the deception when we are confronted in our errors is very serious. When Jesus confronted the Pharisees with their errors, He was trying to help them. When pride led them to double down on their errors, He called them hypocrites, whitewashed tombs, and sons of the devil himself. And He said this regarding what we would call evangelism and discipleship:

> *"Woe to you, scribes and Pharisees, hypocrites! For you travel across sea and land to make a single proselyte, and when he becomes a proselyte, you make him twice as much a child of hell as yourselves."* (Matthew 23:15)

Do you fully understand exactly what Jesus is warning about here? False teachers make false converts. They claim to lead them into eternal life with God but in reality they are leading them to eternal damnation. No excuse is given for the ignorant convert. He is not forgiven because he was deceived by a false teacher. Both teacher and student are condemned to hell.

But here is the important thing to remember. Before Jesus came, the Pharisees thought they were doing the right thing and correctly teaching the Word of God. Some were acting out of ignorance, and Jesus was willing to show them their error for their benefit and the benefit of those they taught. But once confronted in their error, the arrogant Pharisees chose to double down with pride instead of genuine humility, and they exposed and convicted their own hearts before God.

If your pastor or church leadership is currently being deceived like the first-century Pharisees, understand they might genuinely love God and think they are doing the right thing. But they have unknowingly been tainted by ignorance or the influence of other false teachers. Respectfully present them with the opportunity to either humbly see and correct their error or choose to act with arrogant defiance and defend their unbiblical positions. Christians and those who lead us must be people of genuine humility, willing to admit we could be wrong about something, willing to confess and correct our errors, and thankful for being confronted gracefully rather that resenting the confrontation.

If church leadership has serious issues with any of these points, it is fair to wonder if they might be straying into American Christianity, forsaking the Word of God for the doctrines and ways of man. The first step is to determine if they are wrong out of ignorance or are knowingly and willingly teaching false doctrines. If your church leadership is willing to sit down and discuss these reformation points with humility and a comprehensive study of God's Word, at least you know leadership is open to ongoing self-assessment. It is important to understand that the vast majority of churches straying into American Christianity did not purposefully make a decision to do so. The subtle deception of Satan, buttressed by corrupt institutions like public education, media, and government, have slowly led these churches into deception. And if leaders of these churches cannot spot things that are deceiving *them*, how can they possibly equip members to reject deception?

As I mentioned earlier, the greatest challenge facing Christians and Christian church leaders is how to discern deception from truth. Without the ability to discern deception from truth we are easy prey for the father of lies, a being of such cunning and evil that he convinced Adam and Eve to forfeit paradise and eternal life with God. None of us is immune to deception.

How do we spot deception and lies when the greatest and most effective liar in history is honing his craft and enlisting the institutions of this fallen world in his fight against Biblical Christianity? How do we spot deception when it is infiltrating American Christianity and some who are teaching the Word have unknowingly been infected already?

Chapter Seven

Questioning Everything

Okay, not *everything* . . . everything *except* the Word of God, the Bible. Actually, go ahead and try to question even the Bible itself. You will find that since God has always existed and will always exist; since He created and sustains all things; since He transcends time, is all knowing, perfectly righteous, just, holy, and never changing; and since He is incapable of lying, then not only must we believe the Bible, but it must also be our sole system for the measurement of truth. To do less than that is to imply that God could be a liar and thus untrustworthy. So test it when you have questions or uncertainties, because if you know how to correctly interpret it by using the Bible to interpret itself, your faith in God and His Word will only grow.

We have discussed the God-given tools to accurately understand and interpret the Bible:

- Causality

- Non-contradiction

- How to distinguish between truth, facts, opinions, and deception

- Applying biblical conjunctives

For greater depth on these issues please see *The Death of Christian Thought*. We now turn our attention to how we can use the Word of

God to present the gospel to lost sinners, make deeper disciples for Jesus Christ, and how we can help professing Christians who are being deceived to come into the truth of God and come out of man-made gospels and doctrines leading them to eternal hell, or at the least, rendering them ineffective in sharing the gospel with the lost and serving God.

I cannot stress enough that we must understand the power of the deception Satan is promoting through worldly institutions and that none of us is above being deceived. We must remember this when we challenge what is happening in American Christianity and its leadership. I do not believe for a minute that the majority of leaders of American Christianity are intentionally deceiving their church members. Certainly there are some intentional deceivers, but the vast majority of American Christianity leaders are under a spell of deception and actually think they are doing the right things in their churches. Eve probably thought she was doing the right thing when she listened to and obeyed the Serpent. Satan is that clever and deceptive. He adds or changes a single word and turns truth on its ear. A subtle redefining of a single word can lead us into deception that can jeopardize our eternal souls. A subtle redefinition of a particular word can lead us to accept as correct the exact *opposite* of the intended definition of that word. This is how, over time, lies come to be seen as truth.

Understand this: American Christianity is *not* a less-effective, slightly flawed, lesser version of Biblical Christianity; it is the *opposite* of Biblical Christianity! It addresses effects, not causes. It is self-contradictory instead of non-contradictory, and it presents opinions and deception as truth. And realize one more thing that should provide for incredible grace when we interact with others, Christians and non-Christians alike: only by the grace of God does any of us come out of darkness and into the light of Jesus Christ and His Word. The moment we act with pride or arrogance, thinking we are something special, we diminish God and what He has done for us. But for the grace of God we would be lost and completely blinded by the world and its ally American Christianity.

The model in American Christianity for sharing the gospel and making disciples is so flawed it cannot help but be ineffective. It starts with desiring the benefits of salvation in the gospel without accepting the responsibilities. It desires heaven without individual holiness, and blessings without challenges and persecution. So it is built on shifting sands or is like the seed on rocky ground that shoots up early but withers when the troubles of this world bear down on it. American Christianity, with its focus on nickels and noses, redefines what a successful church should look like: a church of many people but little spiritual depth, contrasted with the call for God's church to be holy and peculiar compared to the world. It fails to make true disciples of Jesus who are equipped to share the gospel and answer the difficult questions and accusations people of the world will throw our way because of the fear of looking foolish or unloving. This only serves to render American Christianity churches impotent to help lost sinners come into the light of truth. It has become a stumbling block to those who desire to know God and the gospel of reconciliation.

American Christianity might casually suggest its members go out and share the gospel with family and friends, but the leaders are not equipping members to do so effectively because the leaders often do not even know the gospel themselves. The gospel in American Christianity is a fake, powerless gospel. Where are the calls for confession and sorrowful repentance for our sins against God? Where are the sermons teaching that the wrath of God will one day soon be poured out on all the earth and its people, with only the true disciples of Jesus being spared from it? Where are the teachings of Jesus that if we claim to be His disciples we obey everything He commands of us? When we are armed with a powerless, counterfeit gospel it is little wonder the world makes us look foolish and renders us ineffective in delivering our message.

> "But woe to you, scribes and Pharisees, hypocrites! For you shut up the kingdom of heaven against men; for you neither go in yourselves, nor do you allow those who are entering to go in. Woe to you, scribes and Pharisees, hypocrites! For you devour widows' houses, and for a pretense make long prayers. Therefore you will receive greater condemnation. Woe to you, scribes and Pharisees, hypocrites! For you travel land and sea to win one proselyte, and when he is won,

you make him twice as much a son of hell as yourselves."
(Matthew 23:13-15 NKJV)

American Christianity, by refusing to preach the full counsel of God's Word and replacing biblical doctrine with man-made doctrine, is repeating the hypocrisy of the Pharisees of Jesus' time. It is creating a vicious cycle that plays right into the hands of our enemy. It uses things of this world to lure people to their church and presents a false, worldly gospel that creates false converts with a false sense of eternal security who then share this false gospel with others. This is simply spiritual malpractice, whether done purposefully for gain or unconsciously due to ignorance of God and His Word. Just as Jesus chastised the Pharisees, we are sharing a gospel that turns people into children of hell itself (Matthew 23:15). But again, this is not always conscious malpractice. It is often an effect of those in charge learning from others who were deceived, combined with a lack of zeal to pursue truth from its only source: God and His Word. So always be full of truth *and* grace, willing to consider that others may have been deceived rather than being blatant deceivers.

Let's study ways to improve our communication with others, setting the table for productive discussions with believers and unbelievers alike. Remember that our goal in confronting error must always be to help the other person discover truth and not to show ourselves as more righteous or holy. It all starts with the words we use and how we choose to define them. God used specific words with specific definitions in His Word, and to show ourselves as approved workers of God we must use and teach the words He uses, correctly interpreting and applying His Word (2 Timothy 2:15).

The Power of Redefining Words

Almost every argument I have witnessed between two sincere people who really want to resolve any differences comes from the same sources:

- Either they are using the same word and applying different definitions to that word, or

- They are using two different words with the same exact definition and it is causing confusion between them.

The English language is a sloppy language in many respects when compared to Hebrew and Greek. For example, we have one definition for the word *love*, while in the Bible the Greek word has three different and distinct definitions. Here is a powerful example from God's Word that clearly speaks to a crucial problem in American Christianity:

> *When they had finished breakfast, Jesus said to Simon Peter, "Simon, son of John, do you love me more than these?" He said to him, "Yes, Lord; you know that I love you." He said to him, "Feed my lambs." He said to him a second time, "Simon, son of John, do you love me?" He said to him, "Yes, Lord; you know that I love you." He said to him, "Tend my sheep." He said to him the third time, "Simon, son of John, do you love me?"* (John 21:15-17)

The word Jesus used in questioning Peter's love was *agapao*: consciously choosing to love Jesus with all his heart and mind more than anything else. Peter's affirmation of his love was *phileo*: a love of friendship. The love of Jesus in American Christianity resembles more *phileo* than *agapao*. Jesus is often viewed as a friend who will bail us out when we need Him rather than the One we are to love more than anyone or anything. The love of Jesus in American Christianity is subverted by the unwillingness to surrender and submit to His will above ours. Jesus is presented as something you add to your life instead of becoming your reason for life itself.

Imagine the confusion if Jesus and Peter were speaking in English. It would look more like an Abbott and Costello comedy routine than a teaching from the Bible. But Jesus had to ask Peter the same question three times because He knew Peter was using a different word for *love* than He was using.

If you say to a group of your Christian friends, "I love prostitutes," their response might prove quite interesting and insightful. The ones that scream at you and call you a sinner are hearing and speaking in the language of the world. The ones that ask, "Could you tell me what *kind* of love you have for prostitutes?" (*agape, phileo*, or *eros*) might have a much better grasp on God's language in the Bible.

The world has successfully subverted the definitions of words to defeat our arguments and intimidate, manipulate, and control us. Words like *love, tolerance, marriage, fairness,* and *justice* have been redefined by society to silence the truth. In American Christian churches words like *love, grace, submission, repentance,* and even *marriage* have been watered down to the point that they lose their biblical meaning, focus, and perspective. American Christianity is on the fast track to adopting the world's meanings for these crucial words as it abandons biblical truth for compromise with the world. Because it is speaking the language of culture and not of God it will attract people, but it will fail to make true Christian disciples. It will grow in numbers but not in spiritual depth, eventually looking exactly like the world.

In order to understand the Bible, or anything in this world, it is of paramount importance that we get one truth right. This truth is so profound that every other truth is fully dependent on it. If we get this foundational truth wrong it is almost impossible to get anything right. Yet this foundational truth is being rewritten in American Christianity to placate the world and grow the corporate structure of American Christianity.

Who Is God?

This is the foundational truth upon which rests an understanding of everything else in this world, including being able to correctly interpret God's Word and share it with others. Yet when I meet with professing Christians who have questions or problems in life, it is sad how many of them know a different God from the one in the Bible. This leads to Christians being disillusioned when they do not understand God's nature and character. When we cannot understand how God's righteous and just nature perfectly intersect with His mercy, love, and grace, we are open to deception. Many Christians have suddenly come to think that homosexuality or gender confusion is fine with God because they have homosexual family members or friends who are very nice people and claim to believe in God. This is reconciling God to sinful man, which is the exact opposite of the true gospel of reconciliation.

In an earlier chapter we used the Bible to know God's eternal nature and character. Until we get this truth right, nothing else will make sense. God is the same yesterday, today, and forever. He never changes; we are the ones who need to change. Once you have mastered God's definition of who He is (His nature and character), you can begin to understand His Word.

"Yes, I'm a Christian!"

I am blessed that hundreds of times in my radio career people have knocked on my door asking for help with life's concerns, seeking some wisdom or encouragement from God's Word. I started noticing a pattern a few years ago in many of those who would come to me. No matter what advice I gave some of them from God's Word they would not follow it, and their problems would only get worse over time. As I was writing my previous book, *The Death of Christian Thought,* I was discovering the power of asking people questions instead of assuming I knew everything about them. So when people would come to me seeking advice I would first tell them I wanted to get to know them better so I could be of more help. I asked them if I could ask a few questions.

The first question I always start out with is: "Are you a born-again Christian?" When they answered in the affirmative I would ask them to define that for me. Here is how these encounters often go once I ask that question:

Answer: "I believe in Jesus."

My respectful counter: "But Satan believes that Jesus is God so there must be more to it."

Their next answer: "I believe that Jesus Christ died for my sins."

My respectful counter: "But Satan believes that Jesus died for the sins of man, and he is not a born-again believer, so there must be more."

Answer: "I have accepted Jesus as my personal savior."

My respectful answer: "Please read Romans 10:9 for me and share what it says."

*Because, if you confess with your mouth that Jesus is Lord
and believe in your heart that God raised him from the
dead, you will be saved. (Romans 10:9)*

Here we see the tragic effects of American Christianity. People are
being taught that Jesus is our *savior*, but not the truth that He is also
to be worshiped as *Lord* over all things, including our lives. American
Christianity touts the benefits of salvation while ignoring the responsibilities. It wrongly teaches that we can maintain our stubborn streak
of independence instead of totally surrendering to the lordship of Jesus
Christ. It actually encourages continued rebellion against God by promoting a partial and deceptive gospel that appeals to our flesh.

What Is Our Source for Truth?

Another powerful and effective question to ask people is: "When you
do not know the answer to an important question, where do you turn
for truth?" This is a vital question that will help you determine whether
you are dealing with Christians or unbelievers. Here are some of the
answers I have received when asking people this question:

- "My heart"
- "My gut reaction"
- "My best friend"
- "My pastor"
- "The Internet"

No matter which of these answers is given, I follow up with this question:
"Have they ever been wrong, even just once?" Of course their answer is
yes. I then calmly ask them, "Then how do you know they will not be
wrong the next time"? Unless they are completely deceived, this will
cause them to pause and reconsider their source for truth. If they are
an unbeliever, it is an opportunity to share with them why you search
God's Word for truth and why you can depend on it. If they claim to
be a believer, it is an opportunity to teach them something important
that their church leaders might be failing to teach them about God
and His Word.

The Unbeliever

When an unbeliever asks me why I trust the Bible for truth, here is how I respond:

When I was younger, I realized there had to be a God as I looked around all creation and saw the beauty and majesty of this world. I realized something greater than me had to have created all this. So I started checking out different religions and their beliefs. I found out the Bible is the only reliable source to understand God and all His creation. The Bible teaches us how the world was created and about the God that created and sustains it. It tells us why there is so much pain and sorrow in this world and how that was never God's plan to begin with until man, who had been created by God and given a free will, was given a choice to love and obey God or to do things his way by rebelling against God.

The God who created man wants to reconcile us back to where He created us to live forever: in eternal paradise with Him with no pain or death. God gave us His Word, the Bible, so we could know Him and His plan to reconcile us back to Himself. How do I know it is truth?

- The Bible lays out God's nature and character in a completely non-contradictory explanation. Every other god that has been written about by man is self-contradictory and does not explain how the world was created and why we have so many serious problems.

- The Bible has proven it is reliable by accurately predicting future events hundreds and thousands of years before they happened. It has never once been wrong. And it gives future predictions that we can see unfolding right before us now.

- The Bible gives us the hope we all want: to live forever

in peace and full of joy. And it tells mankind how this can be accomplished. It gives us the eternal hope we so desperately seek.

If you have an adequate understanding of biblical apologetics, you are now in a position to answer the sincere questions of the unbeliever if they truly are seeking God. And you don't need to worry about being able to answer every question they have because the Holy Spirit in you will guide you every step of the way. You will find yourself right where God wants you: being His ambassador delivering His gospel message. Whether the person decides to listen and follow the message is between him and God, but you will have faithfully done what Jesus asked us to do in Matthew 28:19-20, the Great Commission.

If what I shared above seems overwhelming or intimidating to you, it is because American Christianity has so confused the message of the Bible that it seems complex to us, when in reality it is a simple message: a perfect God wants to reconcile sinful, rebellious men back into a right standing with Him, living in perfect peace and harmony forever. This is exactly what almost every human being desires, regardless of their personal or political philosophy! We have the only true answer for a world's quest for peace, harmony, and perfection.

But know and understand this: Only God can do the reconciling. Our human efforts to save anyone will go nowhere, and may actually impede the work of God. So relax and be confident in God, knowing His Word never comes back void. It will either save or condemn every man on judgment day. Deliver His message calmly as His ambassador. Look for opportunities and pray for those God sends your way, and be patient and wait on God to move in their hearts and minds. We are not salesmen who try to close a sale. We are passionate messengers who deliver the message faithfully and wait on God to close the deal.

The Professing Believer

The Barna Group research findings we covered earlier show how confused and deceived those who follow American Christianity have become. The constant thread in the contradictory beliefs expressed throughout the findings is this: Many professing Christians either do not understand

God's Word or do not believe it is truth. There can be no other explanations. These are the sad effects of the growth of American Christianity that deep down worships self over God. It is the unstated belief that we can pick and choose the characteristics of God that we like and dismiss those we do not like, and that we can choose to obey what we want to obey and disregard the rest of God's commands.

This can only lead to one outcome: spiritual confusion. And this is exactly what the Barna Group research shows is happening in American Christianity. Why are so many professing Christians leading lives of despair and defeat? Why are so many on anti-depression medication or seeking help from humanist psychology when life seems overwhelming to them? (I am not saying being on anti-depression medication is a sin nor that it might never be necessary. But in many instances it can be avoided if we understand the Bible and trust in it.)

Why do we keep looking for happiness in things of this world instead of finding peace in all circumstances in God? Why do we not find the joy in suffering that Paul experienced and taught about? Why do we cringe when we hear we have come down with cancer? I realize that last question might seem callous, but if we truly believe what the Bible teaches about earthly death and eternal life for those who trust fully in Jesus Christ, why would we fear earthly death?

When I have met with Christians who are struggling in their marriage or with any issues of this world I ask them a couple questions:

- Do you consider yourself a born-again believer, and if so, how would you define that?

- Where do you turn for truth when you need a serious question answered?

First, it is sad how many who profess to be born-again believers cannot even define what that means. Granted, the Word of God does not have a single verse that defines what "born again" really means, but it is not difficult to determine when we take the time to understand God's Word. A starting point is this: God is right and every man is some combination of right and wrong, and the Bible is the inspired Word of a God who cannot lie. Therefore, if I think I am correct about something but the Bible clearly refutes my assumption, then I need to be humble enough to confess my wrong beliefs and change my mind about them (repentance).

Remember that at least 75 percent of the respondents in the Barna survey who claim to be born-again believers held one or more beliefs contradictory to God's Word. So it is important that once a person has self-identified as a born-again believer we have an objective way to honestly assess their claim for their benefit. Remember what Paul said here?

> *Indeed, all who desire to live a godly life in Christ Jesus will*
> *be persecuted, while evil people and impostors will go on*
> *from bad to worse, deceiving and being deceived. But as for*
> *you, continue in what you have learned and have firmly*
> *believed, knowing from whom you learned it and how from*
> *childhood you have been acquainted with the sacred writ-*
> *ings, which are able to make you wise for salvation through*
> *faith in Christ Jesus. All Scripture is breathed out by God*
> *and profitable for teaching, for reproof, for correction, and*
> *for training in righteousness, that the man of God may be*
> *complete, equipped for every good work.* (2 Timothy 3:12-17)

This is not to say or imply that misled Christians are evil, but it is a clarion warning to how unaddressed deception can lead to greater deception. And Paul gives the solution in verse 16: the Word of God used *for teaching, for reproof, for correction, and for training in righteousness.* If a person is truly born again with the Holy Spirit in them, they will eventually become humbled when confronted with clear error about God's Word, since the Spirit's role is to convict people of the truth. If they reject your heartfelt and graceful correction out of hand it may be a sign that they are not truly born again to begin with. But remember, our goal is to always help others, not to condemn them. So we ask them the second question listed above: Where do you turn for truth when you need a serious question answered?

When you ask this question they will answer with either "The Bible" or perhaps one of the examples we listed above. We discussed how to address a wrong answer above, so let's focus on if they answer correctly by stating, "The Bible." I immediately follow up their correct answer with this question: "Since you rightly acknowledge that the Bible is truth, would you want to know if your beliefs or actions were wrong according to the Bible?" If they answer in the affirmative you have a solid reference point to help them address the problems they are facing.

In a perfect scenario, every time you point out how their question or problem is addressed in the Bible, they will submit to it and change their minds and behaviors, but often that is not the case. They might excuse or justify their wrong actions through one of several objections such as, "Well, that's your interpretation of the Bible!" This is where understanding the biblical principles we shared in correctly interpreting the Word is important so you can gently correct their misunderstandings.

It has been my experience that the majority of self-professed born-again believers really do love God and want to do the right thing, but they have not been trained in how to correctly interpret God's Word so they have no correct starting point to address their errors or problems. They have been slowly indoctrinated into American Christianity where they have been subtly taught that God's Word can have different interpretations and meanings based on individual situations or preferences. But once you get them to state they believe the Bible is always true, and you can subsequently help them to interpret it correctly, you can help them come out from under deception.

This will lead them to one of two eventual places. They will either embrace the truth of God's Word with greater commitment and zeal and see solutions to their questions and problems, or they will revert to their own human understanding and selective application of God's Word. Do not be discouraged if the latter happens. Allow God's Spirit time to work, and pray for them. Resist the temptation to hurry things up and be as patient with them as you would want someone to be with you if you were being deceived. As you continue to meet with them, remember it is always better to ask them questions than to simply make statements of judgment about their responses or failure to grow spiritually. When we ask questions it forces people to think consciously and respond, and we can better ascertain if it is their human understanding or God's Spirit that is influencing their thought process. This is the difference between the human and godly thought process I discuss in *The Death of Christian Thought.*

If they truly are born again and have the Holy Spirit within them, they will be convicted of their errors in God's perfect timing. The Holy Spirit will continue to work on their conscience, aligning it more and more with God and away from their flesh. But this can take time and a patient guide who is willing to let God's Spirit do the convicting instead of us rushing in to be their "savior." If we are seen as the answer to their questions or problems, all we have done is reinforce the illusion of American Christianity that man has all the answers instead of God. We subtly reinforce the very deception many of them were seduced by in the first place.

If they were never really born again to begin with, your sincere questions spoken with grace and truth can be God's instrument to reach them. Remember, our job is to plant the seeds initially and then once they have sprouted, to gently water and mulch the new plant; but the water is God's grace! And only He can give life to the seed to begin with. So be patient with others and understand our role in the process, and never start thinking that our clever words or arguments can save anyone.

Whether dealing with a blatant unbeliever or a person who thinks they are born again but really isn't, eventually you might see that they just continue to reject you as Christ's ambassador. There might come a time when you just have to move on and let God deal with them. Perhaps it is not the love and encouragement of a Christian that they need at this time of their life. Perhaps God will have to allow them to face a crisis so intense that they have nowhere to turn except to Him. Just do what we are commanded to do, being patient ambassadors of Christ who speak the truth with love and grace, and leave the effects to God. And if that crisis hits, they might well come back to you one day seeking help or perhaps God will send them someone else to intervene on His behalf. It doesn't matter as long as the person repents and submits to God. Be prepared to be God's effective ambassador when the opportunity is presented, be a faithful witness to His Word and the gospel, and leave the effects to God. If you try to take on more than God has equipped you to do, it will only lead to either frustration as your message is rejected, or prideful arrogance if the seed does take hold because you will start thinking you actually "saved" someone through your clever human persuasion.

Understand what is accomplished by slowing down and asking important questions to more clearly define the words being used. When we are confronted with truth, a response is required, because as Paul stated in Romans 1, every man has a conscience that knows God exists and knows right from wrong. A person might come to realize he has been taught a false gospel that teaches nothing about submitting our entire life to Jesus as Lord and Master. People might come to realize that American Christianity has deceived them into thinking they are born again when in reality they are not. Once we submit to the lordship of Jesus Christ and fully trust in His Word, everything comes into correct focus because we receive the Holy Spirit who opens our eyes to the truth of the Word and the deception of this world.

But even if the Word of God is rejected, it does not come back void because it will be used to judge all men on judgment day when Jesus returns.

One last piece of advice when we talk with unrepentant sinners or people who believe they are born again but not: Be "contrastive" in your thought process and the words you use. Try to ask questions and listen to their heartfelt responses so you can better understand *why* they believe what they do even if they are wrong. Be humble and always remember that it is only by God's grace that you are not the one under deception. Be patient and do not try to do work only God can do, because it only leads to frustration if they refuse to listen, or to pride if the person actually comes into the light. Our assignment is to speak the truth in love and grace and be prepared to give a reason for the hope we have as true believers, and the rest is up to God.

A Heart for the Lost (Evangelism)

Pray that God gives us a great love for our fellow man made in His image, whether they are unrepentant sinners or professing Christians under deception. May our hearts break over the thought of hearing Jesus speak these words to any man:

"On that day many will say to me, 'Lord, Lord, did we not prophesy in your name, and cast out demons in your name, and do many mighty works in your name?' And then will I declare to them, 'I never knew you; depart from me, you workers of lawlessness." (Matthew 7:22-23)

Evangelism must become a passion for us as God's people. It is God's desire that lost people come to saving faith in Jesus Christ and spend eternity with Him. We as believers have been blessed with the privilege of being His instruments for sharing the gospel of reconciliation.

*Therefore, if anyone is in Christ, he is a new creation. The old has passed away; behold, the new has come. All this is from God, who through Christ reconciled us to himself and gave us the ministry of reconciliation; that is, in Christ God was reconciling the world to himself, not counting their trespasses against them, and entrusting to us the message of reconciliation. Therefore, we are ambassadors for Christ, God making his appeal through us. We implore you on behalf of Christ, **be reconciled to God**. For our sake he made him to be sin who knew no sin, so that in him we might become the righteousness of God.* (2 Corinthians 5:17-21, emphasis added)

Understand what is happening in American Christianity. Instead of sinful men being reconciled to God, people are being taught that salvation is some sort of compromise between man and God. Even its members who are serious about sharing the gospel with lost people are bringing a pea shooter to a knife fight because the gospel preached in these churches is a powerless gospel that cannot convict men of their sinful, wretched, and condemned standing before a holy God. They are being armed with a powerless false gospel incapable of saving anyone, even themselves, and God's holy name and Word are put to public ridicule by a world out to undermine His sovereignty. They eventually get frustrated in their efforts and quit. But American Christianity has a "solution" to this problem. Let's get them to church so they can be saved.

Seeker-Friendly Church and Message

The seeker-friendly church movement is a prime example of how a word or phrase can be twisted slightly and become meaningless or even destructive. The question we must ask is this: Was Jesus seeker friendly? The answer is yes, but we have redefined exactly what that seeker friendliness looked like. American Christianity says Jesus invites people to "come as you are." But Jesus' message was, "Yes, come as you are in your filth and sin, but do not stay that way! Let your faith and trust in Me change you!" This is like preaching on John 3:16-17 while ignoring the next two verses. It gives a partial message that is deceptive and contradicts the Bible. Jesus invited sinners to come to Him, believe and trust in Him, and then stop persistently sinning, which leads us to another word from the Bible that American Christianity has redefined to the detriment of its members.

Grace

Let me be clear. We are saved solely by the grace of God through confession, repentance, and complete faith and trust in who Jesus Christ is and what He accomplished on the cross. No work of man can save us, period. But what is the role of God's grace in the life of a believer? Is its purpose solely to save us from hell?

> For the grace of God has appeared, bringing salvation for all people, training us to renounce ungodliness and worldly passions, and to live self-controlled, upright, and godly lives in the present age, waiting for our blessed hope, the appearing of the glory of our great God and Savior Jesus Christ, who gave himself for us to redeem us from all lawlessness and to purify for himself a people for his own possession who are zealous for good works. Declare these things; exhort and rebuke with all authority. Let no one disregard you. (Titus 2:11-15)

> What good is it, my brothers, if someone says he has faith but does not have works? Can that faith save him? If a brother or sister is poorly clothed and lacking in daily food,

and one of you says to them, "Go in peace, be warmed and filled," without giving them the things needed for the body, what good is that? So also faith by itself, if it does not have works, is dead. (James 2:14-17)

American Christianity, in its zeal for growth, has diminished God's definition of the very word that we stake our claim of forgiveness and salvation upon: grace. The subtle but crucial difference between the Bible's and American Christianity's definitions of grace is this:

- American Christianity defines grace *solely* as the instrument through which we are saved, disregarding its necessary sanctifying work in our lives that leads us to increased holiness.

- The Bible says in the verses above that good works and bearing fruit is a *required effect* of the grace that saves us. In other words, the same grace that saves us (its *cause*) transforms us into a life of increased holiness and good works (the necessary *effect of its cause*). Without an effect there is no real cause.

This is why understanding God's principle of causality is crucial to understanding and living His Word. The *same grace* that saves us is also transforming us into the image of Jesus. And while that transformation happens at various speeds in individuals, if a transformation is not present then there is no true grace.

True Christians become more right over time. God's Word and Spirit through His grace teach us the truth about issues like sexuality, abortion, and gender. Deception makes us more wrong over time. We justify our sins instead of being convicted of them. Is American Christianity becoming more right or more wrong over time? The answer is obvious.

Love

We covered how the New Testament has three different definitions for the word *love* because there are three different words for *love*. American Christianity not only fails to distinguish between them but also confuses people by inaccurately portraying one for another. The social justice gospel is portrayed as unconditional agape love, when in reality it is a selfish love done out of being ashamed of the gospel that can save a man for eternity. We pat ourselves on the back for our love and compassion for the poor, but in failing to share the eternal Bread of Life with them we actually help facilitate their separation from God in hell because deep down we are ashamed of Jesus' words and afraid we will be seen us narrow-minded or judgmental.

Our worldview is the impetus for most of the important decisions we make in life. Many proponents of the social justice gospel believe that once man makes the world a better place economically and environmentally, Jesus then returns to assume His throne. A biblical worldview says that while we are to be kind to others and good stewards of this planet, the world will continue to deteriorate physically, morally, and spiritually because of sin and its effects until Jesus returns in final judgment, destroys this world, and creates a new heaven and earth.

So to help determine if they are deceivers promoting the social justice non-gospel, or simply deceived into believing that helping the poor is more important to God than sharing the gospel, I ask them this question: "What does Jesus do when He returns and what does the world look like just before His return?" Their answer reveals their worldview and if it is an unbiblical worldview I can use the Word of God to gently correct and teach them. It almost always comes down to how people view God's nature and character, along with how we interpret the Bible. And unless we get these two crucial issues correct, we will get nothing else right.

Agape love always looks at bearing long-term fruit and benefits instead of taking shortcuts that may start out good but have no lasting, positive effects. Helping a person with their physical needs without sharing the gospel and pointing them to the truth about God, and the eventual judgment every man will face, bears no lasting fruit and may even impede a lost person's desire to spend eternity with God instead of in hell, because they are being conditioned to trust in man instead of God for solutions.

Liberals tout themselves as people of great tolerance, but when we see their words and actions once their agenda is questioned, we see they are anything but tolerant. Why do liberals fight against the possibility of one innocent person being unjustly sentenced to death while they passionately support the murder of more than one million children every year who committed no crime whatsoever? Why do people who believe in abortion get so angry when someone disagrees with them? Why do liberals take to attacks of personal destruction against anyone who disagrees with them instead of defending their position with logic and reasoning? Because the liberal worldview is fraught with contradiction and God's Word is non-contradictory.

*For the wrath of God is revealed from heaven against all ungodliness and unrighteousness of men, who by their unrighteousness **suppress the truth. For what can be known about God is plain to them, because God has shown it to them**. For his invisible attributes, namely, his eternal power and divine nature, have been clearly perceived, ever since the creation of the world, in the things that have been made. So they are without excuse. For although they knew God, they did not honor him as God or give thanks to him, **but they became futile in their thinking, and their foolish hearts were darkened**. Claiming to be wise, they became fools, and exchanged the glory of the immortal God for images resembling mortal man and birds and animals and creeping things. **Therefore God gave them up in the lusts of their hearts to impurity**, to the dishonoring of their bodies among themselves, because they exchanged the truth about God for a lie and worshiped and served the creature rather than the Creator, who is blessed forever! Amen.*

For this reason God gave them up to dishonorable passions. *For their women exchanged natural relations for those that are contrary to nature; and the men likewise gave up natural relations with women and were consumed with passion for one another, men committing shameless acts with men and receiving in themselves the due penalty for their error.*

And since they did not see fit to acknowledge God, **God gave them up to a debased mind to do what ought not to be done. They were filled with all manner of unrighteousness, evil, covetousness, malice. They are full of envy, murder, strife, deceit, maliciousness. They are gossips, slanderers, haters of God, insolent, haughty, boastful, inventors of evil, disobedient to parents, foolish, faithless, heartless, ruthless. Though they know God's righteous decree that those who practice such things deserve to die, they not only do them but give approval to those who practice them.** (Romans 1:18-32, emphasis added)

Many liberals and anarchists are acting in an insane manner because God has turned them over to a reprobate mind. Their conscience knows the truth about God but their sinful nature has convinced them that it is *not* truth and they live in a state of growing contradiction where fantasy and delusion become reality to them. I covered this in my last book. God did not design the human brain to accept contradictions. When left unresolved they result in mental illness and often psychotic thoughts and behaviors. We are witnessing this in America; and American Christianity, because it does not teach the full counsel of God's Word and wants the love and acceptance of the world to grow their churches, is feeding into this growing insanity to placate the world and keep their doors open.

When liberals nominate a Supreme Court justice who supports abortion and a pro-life senator dares raise any concern whatsoever, they are chastised and told the only qualification for a justice is experience and judicial temperance. But when a justice is nominated and there is even a hint that he or she might lean pro-life, liberals will go to any extent to professionally discredit and personally destroy the nominee. Judicial temperance is no longer a necessary qualification because abortion is at stake! Confront a committed radical liberal with this contradiction and they will revert to name-calling and character assassination because their true father is Satan, the father of lies.

Truth in Love and "Pearls before Pigs"

Once we accept God's definitions for His words and start living accordingly we have the anchor of truth in our lives. We will not be easily deceived by clever lies and opinions. By the power of God's Word and Spirit we should be able to spot deception and confront it for the benefit of others. The Bible instructs us to love all people and share the gospel with those still blinded to the truth of God. We speak the truth full of love and grace, hoping to help lost sinners see their need for Jesus Christ. But Jesus also warned us of this:

> *"Do not give dogs what is holy, and do not throw your pearls*
> *before pigs, lest they trample them underfoot and turn to*
> *attack you."* (Matthew 7:6)

And remember what Paul said in Romans 1: when people consciously reject the truth of God, He turns them over to a reprobate mind to say and do unthinkable evil. This creates a dilemma for Christians in when and how we interact with lost sinners and fake Christians. How can we know if people have been turned over to a reprobate mind and are beyond the saving grace of God because of their conscious rejection of Him? When do we decide to heed Jesus' command to no longer cast pearls before pigs?

This is a very delicate and difficult decision, and one we should never take lightly. We should always give people the benefit of the doubt and not assume they are of a reprobate mind unless the evidence is clear. Since only God knows the future and the heart of every person, we must tread with humility and compassion on this subject. But the Bible indicates that we should be able to spot what Jesus called *pigs*; otherwise, He would not have commanded us to not give them sacred things (His Word). So how can we best determine if someone is still open to the truth of God or if they have been turned over to their evil ways because they have consciously rejected God? We will explore some ways we can make an informed decision, but always remember, heartfelt prayer before God is always our first step.

The world, and sadly, American Christianity, has twisted the definitions of words to oppose God and advance their worldly agenda. Remember, to be shown as a worker approved by God rightly interpreting and applying His words is the requirement laid out. Here are some key words the world is redefining to fit into their evil agenda:

Tolerance

The dictionary defines *tolerance* as "the ability or willingness to tolerate something, in particular the existence of opinions or behavior that one does not necessarily agree with."

First, understand this: God is not tolerant but He is patient. His grace and mercy are patient, giving sinful men every opportunity to confess and repent before He weighs in with His eternal judgment that will determine where every man spends eternity. But when we stand before Him in judgment He will not be tolerant of unrepentant sin.

Christians should be patient and tolerant with those who disagree with God. No committed Christian believes adulterers or homosexuals should be put to death or be put in prison for their beliefs or actions. When we interact with unbelievers in our neighborhood or at work, we should respect them and even acknowledge their right to believe whatever they want to believe about God.

Radical liberals consider themselves the most tolerant people and paint Christians as intolerant. But by the definition of tolerance, the exact opposite is true:

- Christians believe that homosexuals and people struggling with gender confusion should be loved even though their lifestyles oppose God's Word. The world is saying more and more boldly that there is no place for people who think homosexuality is a sin or that there are only two genders created by God.

- Biblical Christians believe in forgiveness, no matter how offensive the crime. Liberals are incapable of true forgiveness. They dig into the ancient history and actions of anyone who opposes their agenda, even lying to punish anyone that stands in their way. One "mistake" and you will be destroyed, and that includes any opinion you have *ever* stated that contradicts their worldview.

- Christians are taught to love their friends and enemies. The world uses "friends" to advance their agenda but will quickly turn on them if they dare ever stand in the way of their increasingly radical agenda. Liberals also seek to destroy their enemies.

When we can point out these contradictions gracefully, we can start to determine if the person is humble and willing to consider another perspective. If they are not, they may be approaching the state of a "reprobate mind" where even when confronted with obvious contradictions in their stated values and beliefs they double down on their deception and faulty beliefs.

Bigot, Homophobe, Misogynist, and Racist

If you dare mention anything from God's Word that discusses homosexuality, slavery, or women, brace yourself because you are certain to be accused of being one or more of these four things. And if you think your historic behavior that refutes these wild accusations will prove your innocence, sit down and have a talk with Judge Kavanaugh. You will be destroyed if you dare state any opinion or cite any biblical truth that contradicts the insanity of this increasingly liberal, self-worshiping world. But let's look at the dictionary's definition of each of these words to see who is really guilty of these accusations.

Bigot: "a person who is intolerant toward those holding different opinions." Biblical Christians believe that homosexuality is a sin but that homosexuals should be treated with respect because they are human beings made in the image of God. We love them enough to share the truth of God's Word with them, but even if they reject it we respect them and are kind to them, even providing for their needs when they arise. We are good neighbors and even friends with them.

Liberals, bolstered by the weakness of American Christianity, are the real bigots, because if you disagree with their opinions *you* are called a hateful bigot no matter what your actions show. Their actions prove they are the exact evil they accuse Christians of being, but because the definition of the word has been twisted, Christians stand guilty in the court of public opinion as bigots.

Homophobe: "a person with an extreme and irrational aversion to homosexuality and homosexual people." The Bible teaches us to love and be kind to all people. It teaches us that *all* sin is an affront to God, not just homosexuality. It teaches us that the hypocritical professing Christians who judge the eternal salvation of homosexuals while secretly practicing adultery and justifying it will be judged harshly by Jesus. Biblical Christians are instructed to hate sin but always love the sinner.

The world is teaching people to hate anyone who is a sinner in *their* eyes. Heterosexual people are being marginalized as having antiquated beliefs and are classified as "Neanderthals." Liberals are the *heterophobes* who have an irrational fear of us and see us as a threat so severe that we must be silenced at all costs.

As a baseball fan of the Milwaukee Brewers I was saddened when in the middle of a 2018 pennant race, the rival Chicago Cubs traded for an excellent baseball player by the name of Daniel Murphy. Back in March 2015, Murphy, then a member of the New York Mets, was asked about former baseball player Billy Bean, who is openly gay and now serves as the Ambassador for Inclusion for the league. Murphy called being gay a "lifestyle" and said, "I disagree with his lifestyle. I do disagree with the fact that Billy is a homosexual. That doesn't mean I can't still invest in him and get to know him. I don't think the fact that someone is a homosexual should completely shut the door on investing in them in a relational aspect. Getting to know him. That, I would say, you can still accept them but I do disagree with the lifestyle, one hundred percent."

Murphy, a devout Christian, was not ready to walk back on those comments, even three years later as he sat in front of the Chicago media when he became a Chicago Cub. When asked to clarify his comments and asked if he has changed his stance, Murphy said this: "What I would say to that is that I've been able to foster a really positive relationship with Billy Bean since that time. I'm really excited to continue to cultivate that relationship that we've built. Billy, his job I think as Ambassador for Inclusion with Major League Baseball is a vital role so that everyone feels included, not only in our industry in baseball, but in all aspects of life."

In spite of this, Murphy was branded a homophobe and several people publicly called for the Cubs to terminate their association with him. Understand what happened here. Murphy, a devout Christian, stated his belief that homosexuality is wrong according to God, but that in no way should it hinder his becoming friends with a practicing homosexual or should the fact that a person is a homosexual ever hinder that person from having an important position in baseball. Please tell me how that justifies calling Murphy a homophobe. But that is what evil does; it constantly moves the bar on what is acceptable in order to advance its agenda. So who are the real "intolerants" when it comes to sexual lifestyles?

Misogynist: "a person who dislikes, despises, or is strongly prejudiced against women." Now we must explore the inverse of this. The Oxford Dictionary defines the word *misandrist* as a person who views men the same as a misogynist views women: with spite and strong prejudice. Both of these of course are unbiblical and destructive and should not be tolerated in any civil society. But which one is more prevalent in our nation? You can find hundreds of articles condemning all men as "pigs" and "lowlifes," but you will need to search very hard for even one article condemning all women in a similar manner. The Me Too movement is gaining power because it is backed by the belief that "women don't lie about these things." That of course infers that any man who would refute a woman's claim that he sexually harassed her would have to always be lying. So who are the ones with a dislike and spite for, and strong prejudice against, an entire sexual class? It is liberals and radical feminists, and because the American Christian church panders to these two movements so the church can increase in numbers, men have become a pariah in the eyes of secular society.

Racist: "a person who shows or feels discrimination or prejudice against people of other races, or who believes that a particular race is superior to another." Racism, as it is portrayed by the world, does not really exist. The Bible teaches that there are different "tribes and tongues" but that there is only one human race and all are descendants of the same sinful father and mother, Adam and Eve. The differences in our skin pigment and other distinguishing physical characteristics are a result of the migration of different people groups after the great flood. Genesis 10 gives the account of Noah's descendants spreading across the earth, starting in Africa and Asia.

Judging a man or woman based on their skin tone is just an excuse for hating other people who are also made in the image of God. And while sadly our nation for too long embraced slavery as a justifiable means of growing the economy, our eyes have been opened to this tragedy and we have made strides to correct this evil treatment of our fellow man. But the pendulum has swung too far the other way as liberals use this issue to advance their agenda of power and control.

Many colleges now offer courses about "white privilege," claiming that racism is worse than ever and that every person should be held accountable for the wrongful actions of ancestors from decades or centuries before we were even born. Black Lives Matter has successfully bullied and intimidated people to the point that if you even say, "All lives matter," you are considered a racist. The racism that does exist in our nation is being advanced by political movements that want to destroy our nation and subsequently undermine the creation account in the Bible that clearly states all men belong to *one* race: the human race created by God. Devaluing people born with *less* skin coloring than others has become the new racism in our nation, and it is every bit as evil as the inverse. So again, liberals have managed to accuse others of exactly what they are guilty of, and if you dare question them you will be personally and viciously attacked and your job will be threatened.

Summary

God's Word uses specific words with exact definitions because God is a God of order. The world, under the dominion of Satan, confuses matters by redefining words to suit its agenda. This should be expected of a world that hates God and presses forward with an antichrist agenda. But when the church becomes sloppy in teaching God's Word, redefining what He means in the words He uses, we are open to confusion and deception. And in its desire to look more like the world so the world will love it, American Christianity has allowed Satan to whisper in its ear and change the definitions of the specific words God uses. This initially sows seeds of confusion, and eventually leads to biblically lazy and illiterate professing Christians adopting beliefs and positions that oppose the God they claim to worship.

Whether talking with other Christians in the pursuit of holiness (sanctification), or reaching out to the lost people of this fallen world, it is vital that we slow down and not get immersed in the confusion authored by the father of lies. Take the time to ask others to clearly define the meaning of the words they use in order to better understand them and produce a solid basis for further discussion.

If you can ask the right questions that cause them to realize how their actions contradict their beliefs, you reach the "moment of truth." If they are willing to confess they were wrong and show a sincere desire to become more right, they might be open to pursuing truth, and we can share the only truth with them: God in His Word. But if they double down and defend their hypocrisy, wanting what they want more than wanting to know the truth, you might be dealing with a Romans 1 reprobate. Do not cast any more pearls before them. You have introduced them to the contradiction that is consuming them. If they are still salvageable in God's eyes, let Him have His way with them. Any attempt to soften what God puts them through might be interrupting the work God is trying to accomplish in their lives to lead them out of blindness.

Chapter Eight

Reestablishing Jesus' Church to Its Original Intent and Process

What Spiritual Legacy Are We Leaving Our Children?

And they devoted themselves to the apostles' teaching and the fellowship, to the breaking of bread and the prayers. And awe came upon every soul, and many wonders and signs were being done through the apostles. And all who believed were together and had all things in common. And they were selling their possessions and belongings and distributing the proceeds to all, as any had need. And day by day, attending the temple together and breaking bread in their homes, they received their food with glad and generous hearts, praising God and having favor with all the people. And the Lord added to their number day by day those who were being saved. (Acts 2:42-47)

Satan used the free will of Adam and Eve to deceive them into thinking they could improve upon what God had created. American Christianity is using our own human wisdom to try to improve upon how Jesus created His church. Look at the four things (causes) Jesus' church devoted itself to in the first century:

- The teachings of the Scriptures

- The breaking of bread (communion)

- Prayer
- A willingness to share all they had with fellow Christians in need

Now let's look at the *effects* of their gathering in fellowship as the Bible instructs:

- Awe came upon every member of the church.
- Many signs and wonders were observed.
- The needs of fellow believers were met by fellow Christians.
- God was continually praised and their fellowship spread to their individual homes and neighborhoods.
- *God* added to their numbers.

When God's people do the right thing (God's cause), God provides wonderful effects! They may not be in our timing or quite as we had hoped, but nonetheless God is always faithful and the early church expanded around the world because they were faithful to God.

But sinful man can never resist trying to improve on God's ways. So American Christianity compromises with sinful culture, embraces a worldly Church Growth Movement, and uses man-made doctrines and traditions to "improve" upon the model Jesus established for His everlasting church. The effects are that American Christianity leads people away from God rather than drawing them nearer to Him.

At the risk of redundancy I will state this important fact once again: American Christianity is not some less-than-perfect replica of Biblical Christianity; it is the opposite of it! God's ways are replaced with man's ways; God's doctrines and traditions are thrown out in favor of man's; and Jesus' model for growing His church is completely reversed in favor of the wisdom of this world. But I am convinced that the majority of church leaders do not intend for this to be happening, and with some subtle but crucial adjustments, any church serious about serving God can return to God's intent for His church.

The Christian church in America is at a dangerous crossroads. Studies show a large majority of Christian youth are disillusioned by what they see in the church and they are leaving at an alarming rate. If we think we face challenges as Bible-believing Christians today, what might happen when today's youth, who are increasingly disillusioned about the Christianity they see, become tomorrow's leaders in our church and nation? By returning to the basics of Biblical Christianity we can develop strong future Christian leaders. But this requires that we admit our failures in allowing the Christian church in America to drift toward secular humanism and embracing secular culture instead of offering an alternative to it.

Here are seven steps that I believe can refocus a church that is drifting from serving God toward serving man, building up future church leaders passionate for God's truth:

Step 1: Unashamedly teach about God's unchanging nature and character

As we discussed earlier, when we pick and choose the characteristics that God gives us to identify His nature and character, everything starts to fall apart in our churches. There is nothing to be ashamed of in teaching His unchanging nature and everything to lose when we diminish it. God's wrath against unrepentant sin and His grace and mercy toward those who have repented are not contradictory in any way. If we use God's love and grace alone to attract people to our churches, we present an incomplete gospel without heartfelt repentance or desire to be made holy as He is holy (1 Peter 1:13-16).

Today's youth want to know truth, but what they are experiencing in American Christianity only confuses them further. This leads to frustration and youth seeking spirituality in all the wrong places, setting up the church to drift further from God with each passing generation. They have legitimate questions we need to answer from God's Word.

Have we become ashamed of God and His Word? Do you find yourself feeling uneasy and unable to explain why God destroyed and killed every person in Sodom, or had Joshua wipe out entire cities of evil people? Do we believe God's Word lacks the power to change hearts and minds? Do we really think human cleverness and compromise is a better way to save souls than the gospel?

Step 2: Teach the complete gospel so people are spiritually transformed by it

We must stop acting ashamed of the gospel by sanding it down to appeal to more people. Proclaim it without shame and let God's Spirit convict the hearts of sinful men. We have been given a great, sacred message to deliver to a fallen world full of people rebelling against God. It is the height of human arrogance and rebellion against God to change the message He wants us to deliver to the lost. Teach the four components of the complete gospel:

- Heartfelt, sorrowful confession of our sinful nature and rebellion against God.

- Heartfelt repentance – a change of mind and heart that leads to a change in behavior.

- Complete faith and trust in who Jesus is and what He accomplished on the cross: the *only* way that sinful man can be reconciled to God. Complete faith and trust includes a strong desire to obey everything He commanded us as the proof that we truly love Him more than anything.

- And when we fully embrace these truths about the gospel, God's Spirit comes to guide us and convict us of the need to be continually transformed into the image of Jesus, evidenced by our beliefs, words, and actions – more and more like Him every day.

And he said to all, "If anyone would come after me, let him deny himself and take up his cross daily and follow me. For whoever would save his life will lose it, but whoever loses his life for my sake will save it. For what does it profit a man if he gains the whole world and loses or forfeits himself? For whoever is ashamed of me and of my words, of him will the Son of Man be ashamed when he comes in his glory and the glory of the Father and of the holy angels. (Luke 9:23-26)

Is American Christianity ashamed of Jesus and His words? If we feel we must water down or soften the gospel He delivered, then yes, it is ashamed of Jesus and His words.

Step 3: Show our youth genuine Biblical Christianity

Jesus established His church to become a pure, spotless bride without blemish (Ephesians 5). This should be the goal of the individual Christian and the church fellowship where we gather and worship. Our younger generations are crying out for real substance in their spiritual journey, and up to 80 percent of them are leaving the Christian faith as public education completes its indoctrination program in college. They are seeing the growing hypocrisy of American Christianity and they want nothing to do with it. Sadly, this leads them to seek spiritual truth and meaning in all the wrong places. These younger people are future leaders in our churches and nation, and unless we can offer them genuine Biblical Christianity instead of American Christianity, their rise to leadership will only perpetuate the slide of apostasy in American Christianity.

They have legitimate questions about social justice, racism, sex and gender, the environment, and raising families in an increasingly dangerous world. They see petty divisions within the church and yet a failure by the church to really stand for anything substantive. They have been lied to by public education, media, corporations, and government. They have been lured into the fantasy that a college degree (from an institution that hates God) will bring them purpose and provide for their families . . . and they graduate with massive debt and little hope. They are witnessing friends commit suicide at an alarming rate for lack of real hope.

God's Word has the right answers to every question they have! But we have failed to teach it to them correctly because we ourselves don't understand it. We can tell them to "read the Bible," but when they do so and ask sincere questions about it, we cannot give them the answers from the very book we point them to. Is it any wonder they grow up jaded and hopeless?

Salvation is our *hope*, but a serious pursuit of holiness gives us *purpose* in our lives, and young people need a purpose. It gives us a goal to shoot for: Becoming more like Jesus Christ every day. Holiness gives us a standard of excellence in a world that tells us there is no standard.

To a growing number of young people, American Christianity has become just another institution that has lied to them, offering them a false hope that leads to despair. Acknowledging and teaching that holiness, not just salvation, is the goal of true Christians gives us both hope and purpose.

Step 4: Teach biblical unity, not human unity

The false unity advanced in American Christianity serves Satan, not God. It eliminates the one element needed for unity: purity of substance. Purity is never something achieved by *adding* ingredients; it is only attained by *eliminating* harmful ingredients. Man-made doctrines do not purify the church, they pollute and stain her. This truth cuts both ways: it opposes the modern-day gnostic who believes that sin no longer matters to God because we have been "saved" (Romans 6:1-4) and the modern legalist who adds human restrictions upon Christians as a requirement for salvation or sanctification (Matthew 23:13-15; 1 Corinthians 6:12).

Biblical church discipline gives us the method to promote real Christian unity that pleases God. The bride of Christ becomes one with Him as we are cleansed of our sin and adultery against Him. It gives us a measuring stick and method to determine when someone is serious about pursuing holiness or is a professing Christian who only wants the benefits of salvation without the responsibilities – fake Christians who sow discord and advance disunity.

Applying biblical conjunctives is a key to correctly understanding the difference between true biblical doctrine and false human doctrine. As we grow in our understanding of these biblical conjunctives, the many arguments we experience about doctrine are resolved and disappear. We are now able to reconcile important issues like these that promote discord in the church:

- Reconciling God's sovereignty and man's free will regarding salvation.

- The role and effects of sin in the Christian life and the topic of eternal security.

- Understanding Jesus' and Paul's teachings reconciling the law and grace. How did Jesus fulfill the law without abolishing it? (This issue addresses the very nature and character of God, and if we cannot understand this conjunctive, we fall for the false teachings of today's emergents who claim God has lowered the standards for man to be saved, promoting universal salvation).

- Understanding the different reasons for Jesus' first and final coming (John 12:47-48).

- The role and responsibility of Christians in judging others (*who* to judge, *why* to judge, *when* to judge, and *how* to judge biblically).

Biblical Christian unity eliminates man-made doctrines, both those that permit unrepentant sin and dangerous false teachings, and those that add human conditions for salvation and sanctification. It allows for mercy and grace with accountability, never allowing grace to become a license to continue sinning. But it also fulfills Paul's teaching that love is patient.

Our youth see through the hypocrisy of American Christianity. They see us claim to believe one thing but then live in a way that contradicts our stated beliefs. By showing them genuine biblical unity around God's doctrines and standards, where Christians find true biblical fellowship and community, we can groom them as the spiritual leaders we will need them to be in the coming years. But if we continue presenting the sham of American Christianity as if it were from God, they will grow more disillusioned and will fulfill their desire for spirituality in ways that condemn their eternal souls.

Step 5: Bring money into proper perspective

American Christianity is built on the foundation that the desires of the customer must be met in order to become a growing, successful church. Everyone loves that "new-car smell," so we buy a new car when the thrill of our current one wears off. People spend close to a thousand dollars for a new smartphone that is only marginally better than the one we spent eight hundred dollars for just one year earlier. When newlyweds in previous times bought their first home, they purchased something functional and affordable, hoping one day years later to be able to afford their "dream home." Today, young couples accumulate massive debt to make their first home their dream home – only to find a couple years later a better, more expensive replacement. And when one of them loses their job or becomes ill, the dream home becomes a financial albatross forcing them into bankruptcy.

American Christianity churches promote the exact same consumer-mindedness. American Christianity has become a "Field of Dreams" ("If you build it, they will come") instead of a house built on the rock of Jesus Christ. It trades substance for fluffy style and comfort. It creates massive debt and financial obligations to build white-washed tombs – beautiful on the outside but rotting within. It falls into the trap of serving money by thinking if they build a new, beautiful church that people will be drawn to it. But then the church down the street builds a newer, more luxurious church and people motivated by their flesh flock to *that* church. So, "Hey, we better respond and build an even bigger, more luxurious church to bring them back!" It uses things that please the flesh to attract people *of* the flesh, falling for the illusion of the Church Growth Movement's definition of success. Whatever you use to attract customers will be what you need to keep doing better to keep them. American Christianity attracts people through the desires of their flesh – and then they are forced to double down on the fleshly appeal to keep them.

And what is the ultimate effect of this Field of Dreams church? It is taken over by people of the flesh, not the Spirit. It becomes as poisonous as drinking salt water, a self-defeating entity that will one day be forced to bow to Antichrist to maintain its prestige and financial stability.

Today's youth are rejecting the greed they see in government and corporations. And they see American Christianity as just another greedy corporation willing to deceive, mislead, and lie for their financial allegiance.

The fellowship Nancy and I belong to (about fifty families) has a zero budget, with no paid staff, no paid pastor, and no massive church building with a huge mortgage. This frees up our elders to teach the Word of God without fear or compromise because:

- There are no financial pressures to maintain or increase the number of members.

- There is no fear of government one day threatening a non-profit status if the church does not submit to man instead of God.

And it frees us as members knowing:

- The Word of God will be preached without compromise or a hidden human agenda.

- We are able to give money to Christian organizations committed to sharing the gospel and making disciples instead of propping up a wasteful, bloated institution that might one day be forced to submit to government.

"No one can serve two masters, for either he will hate the one and love the other, or he will be devoted to the one and despise the other. You cannot serve God and money." (Matthew 6:24)

Take the time to slow down and really take to heart what Jesus is saying here. If you serve (love) money, you *cannot* serve God. When American Christianity sells out to the world by using the god the world worships and serves (money) to attract people to it, irreparable damage is being done to those attracted to this church. They are being taught to serve money instead of God by the very same church that Jesus instructed to teach and do the opposite. American Christianity, perhaps unknowingly, is encouraging and teaching people to worship and serve the false god and master that Jesus warned would actually exclude us from serving Him! This is a dangerous paradox with dangerous ultimate effects. Many will perish for eternity because American Christianity did the exact opposite of what Jesus said we must do. This is why I will continue to remind you that American Christianity is not some slightly flawed version of Biblical Christianity, but rather is the polar opposite.

Step 6: Return to using God's definitions for His words

As we covered earlier, Satan is a master at twisting definitions of words, and his minions of this world are mastering this art of deception quite well. Words like *love* and *tolerance* have been distorted so badly that in some instances their definitions become the exact opposite of the original definitions. Is accepting any behavior or belief system, no matter how self-destructive, really *love*? No, it is the opposite of true love. Tell me how *tolerant* radical liberals are – the people who claim to champion it – these days. If you dare speak out against their cause you will be bullied or beaten into silence and acceptance.

American Christianity is not immune to this redefinition of words either. The definition of grace (God's divine influence and work that saves *and* sanctifies us) has unofficially been redefined to excuse ongoing, unrepentant sin, offering the benefits of salvation without the responsibilities. God's word *faith* is defined this way in His Word: "complete persuasion; moral conviction; complete assurance and fidelity." In American Christianity it has been redefined as mere intellectual belief: Well, I believe Satan exists but I will not put my faith in him!

Likewise, we have allowed the word *church* to be redefined. In the Bible the word used for *church* is *ekklesia*: "a called-out community of faithful Christians."

> "Again I say to you, if two of you agree on earth about
> anything they ask, it will be done for them by my Father in
> heaven. For where two or three are gathered in my name,
> there am I among them." (Matthew 18:19-20)

By the biblical definition, a husband and wife, or a small group of faithful Christian believers gathered, constitutes a "church." *Where* we worship is of no matter to God. *Who* we worship (God alone) and *how* we worship Him (unified in spirit and truth) does matter. So why is it that American Christianity redefines the word *church* to identify it as a place rather than a gathering of committed believers? Could it be to offer the illusion that the building we gather in is more important than the One we are to worship? Could it be to imply that unless you come to this building you cannot draw into the presence of God? Could it be to get us to become dependent on an institution of man instead of God? I do not believe these are conscious reasons for this redefining of this crucial word. But make no mistake concerning the subtle message and danger they convey – that a human institution (American Christianity) is of more importance that a biblical *ekklesia*.

I know a strong believer in Jesus Christ who was ordered by his church elders to stop leading a Bible study with other men he had been leading for years because it was not "authorized" by church leadership. What kind of spiritual pride and insanity is that? They were actually coming against what Christ defined as His church! They also threatened to kick him out of the church for what they called "unrepentant sin" against God for him daring to question the church's allegiance to Willow Creek and their Global Leadership Summit and asking them if this was the example of leadership they wanted members to emulate. This is textbook Purpose Driven Church deception.

All this, it can be argued, is because American Christianity has allowed Satan and the world to redefine God's definition of *church*.

Step 7: Stop confusing political and spiritual issues

The Johnson Amendment of 1954 was introduced with the supposed intent of making certain churches could maintain their tax-exempt status and not wade into political fights and issues. Over time it has become a tool of intimidation against churches that would hold human government accountable to God's righteous decrees. How has this been accomplished? By intimidating church leaders who have allowed spiritual issues to be called "political" and thus off-limits for discussion and teaching within the church.

When we treat issues like abortion, sexual preference, and gender as political issues, we are ceding power to government over God. Immigration, taxation levels, and social welfare can be viewed as political, where true Christians of good conscience can differ in their opinions. But when human life itself and a redefining of marriage and gender are positioned as political instead of spiritual issues, it is nothing short of spiritual malpractice by American Christianity.

Step 8: Understand who Jesus established His church for

Jesus established His church as an *ekklesia*: an assembly of fully committed believers and disciples of Jesus. Not perfect followers who would never sin, but followers who desire perfection in Him through His Word and Spirit, confessing our failures and willing to be held mutually accountable for living a life consistent with our stated beliefs and faith. Jesus, in Matthew 18, and Paul, in 1 Corinthians 5, made it clear that *unrepentant* sinners have no place in the body of Christ. Paul goes so far to say that the unrepentant sinner should be thrown out and *deliver*[ed] . . . *to Satan for the destruction of* [his] *flesh, so that his spirit may be saved in the day of the Lord.* We are told repeatedly that light and darkness have nothing in common, and there is nothing darker than unrepentant sinners. And according to Paul in 1 Corinthians 5, the unrepentant sinner damages the church and the church damages him when it allows him to remain in a state of false security.

In Biblical Christianity sinners who repent and seek holiness are welcome. Unrepentant sinners are welcome to visit the church and hear the gospel preached, but they are not to remain in a state of unrepentant sin as members of the church. American Christianity invites sinners to join and stay even if they do not repent. This disobedience to God's direction is excused as being seeker friendly in the misguided hope that somehow Christianity will miraculously rub off on them by hanging around Christians and hearing the Word of God preached. This is shortsighted thinking because the "Word" preached in many of these churches is a humanized version, watered down to appeal to the flesh rather than the spirit and conscience of fallen sinners, and the lifestyles of American Christians are more like the world than what is taught in God's Word.

> "Woe to you, scribes and Pharisees, hypocrites! For you travel across sea and land to make a single proselyte, and when he becomes a proselyte, you make him twice as much a child of hell as yourselves." (Matthew 23:15)

One important factor in ascertaining if your church leaders seek to be a church of Biblical Christianity or American Christianity is determining what they see as the requirements for membership in the church. Is the church to be comprised solely of repentant sinners seeking holiness? Or does it allow unrepentant sinners to remain and potentially infect the church, hindering its call to spiritual purity?

Personal Testimony

Nancy and I have been so incredibly blessed by becoming members of our Christian fellowship, where Acts 2 is used as the model for Jesus' church. If I were to extensively list the blessings we have experienced there, it would take an entire new book, but I will share the major blessings.

We are challenged and encouraged by the *complete* Word of God, not just select verses that can be manipulated to feed our sinful flesh. God's Word and standards of pursuing perfection for His children remind us of the many times we continue to sin and fall short of His standards for true believers. But we are also reminded of the beauty of His grace and forgiveness in the gospel. So we are drawn closer to God while realizing we were further away than our deceitful human hearts led us to believe. This makes the gospel and God's grace even more amazing as we realize His perfect holiness and our continuing sin; yet He still loves and has forgiven us, and we grow increasingly committed to turning away from our sins!

Our fellowship is guided by elders who are serious about God's requirements and assignments for them. They teach the Word of God and when necessary, confront us if they see words or actions that contradict God's teachings. They also ask us to hold them accountable to the same biblical standard.

We have no paid pastor. (I am *not* accusing any church that has a paid pastor of being unbiblical.) Our church leadership is just concerned that any one man who is elevated to the position of sole teacher of the Word could become puffed up with pride as Christians start to look to him instead of Jesus as the one to follow. We listen to selected sermons from pastors whose theology and messages have been vetted against the Bible by our elders, and then one of the elders will come up afterward and continue expounding upon the message and help us to understand how to apply it to our lives.

We are challenged and equipped to share the gospel with our family, friends, and neighbors instead of just "inviting them to church." The fellowship has a team of evangelists who regularly go to public venues and events sharing the gospel and equipping fellowship members to do the same in our lives.

We are not financially beholden to the government or man. We are not a 501c3 organization so the government could never use that tool to bully us into silence. We have no paid staff and no budget. The couple who own the property where we gather to worship generously takes care of any major expenses and we as members pitch in to provide food for fellowship and assist them in keeping the property maintained and clean.

We are encouraged to give generously to organizations that are sharing the gospel and doing God's work in our community and around the world. Since we have no church budget to support, it allows us to become people of generosity where real needs and opportunities to spread the gospel exist. When fellowship members face an economic challenge or need some major work done, the fellowship has a team of servants who organize people from the fellowship willing and able to assist.

We have men's and women's Bible studies throughout the week. On Sunday mornings one of our men's studies starts at 7:15 and ends at 9:30, and we then head to corporate fellowship where the service usually lasts about two hours, and the Word of God is front and center. It includes a time to commemorate Jesus' sacrifice on the cross through communion and a time of small-group prayer. We end with an hour of food and fellowship, meaning we usually get home between 1:30 and 2:00 p.m. – a seven-hour experience and we cherish every moment of it! I say this not to hold our fellowship up as perfect, because we are far from it and we know it. We are a group of about 100 born-again believers who unfortunately continue to sin as the Holy Spirit convicts us of hidden sin in our hearts, but we seek to be sanctified by God's Word and Spirit with each passing day.

We know we are saved by God's grace alone and completely dependent on Him for anything good that comes out of our lives. But we acknowledge the affront to God that our ongoing sin is and seek more of God's grace and Spirit to conquer our sins, being perfected for the day when each of us joins Jesus as part of His eternal bride.

Summary

It is time for a reality check. Have you ever seen a man or a woman who, instead of aging gracefully, tries to recapture a façade of youth by wearing a bad hair piece, having excessive plastic surgery, or dressing like they are a hip teenager? Instead of embracing their advancing years and sharing accumulated wisdom through experience and learning, they try to act like they are still young and "hip" and only make themselves look foolish. This is how many youth see American Christianity. They are seeing through the deception, confusion, and hypocrisy. They have serious questions that demand truthful answers from God. They are looking to solid Bible-believing Christians who can show them God's answers to their crucial questions about all the problems and confusion in this world. But instead of finding this, they see professing Christians and church leaders who only add to their confusion and cannot point them to truth. They want truthful answers and genuine fellowship and community. Instead, American Christianity feeds into their disdain for the hypocrisy and greed of the world around them. They want a genuine spiritual relationship with God, but American Christianity only gives them more of what this fallen world has to offer: hopelessness and despair. It is time that we grow up as a church and ask God's forgiveness for how we have misrepresented church to our young people and return to the Word of God as our model for Christian fellowship.

Do you belong to the church that Jesus shed His blood for? One that is comprised of a peculiar people that stick out like a sore thumb when compared to this world? One that welcomes sinners to learn of His salvation and grace, hear and fully accept the complete gospel, and then strive to live a life of testimony to God's saving grace? One that follows God and not men? One that teaches the full counsel of God's Word rather than selective verses that can feed our flesh instead of killing it?

Or is your church starting to look more and more like the world every day? Is it adopting ways of this sinful world to be more attractive to people of the flesh? Has it established its own mission instead of striving to carry out Jesus' mission of sharing the gospel and making disciples?

How do you feel as you prepare to go to your church? Do you feel drained and only attend out of obligation? Are you preparing to go to church because you feel you *have* to? Are you worried about what others would think if you did not show up? Would you rather just stay home and get some more sleep? Or do you get excited about gathering in fellowship once again? Are you going because you really want to? Are you praying and asking God to prepare your heart and mind for the message from His Word? Are you excited to learn more about God's Word and how to live it out every day? Do you long for real Christian fellowship, looking for ways to be a blessing to your fellow Christians?

How do you feel and what are you thinking right after your church service? Glad it is over? Beaten down and tired? Feeling like you do after a hard day at work, glad it is over so you can relax and do what you *really* want to do? Or are you energized? Are you grateful for all of God's blessings, yet challenged about your ongoing sin and rebellion against Him? Are you feeling joy *and* conviction? Joy over the blood He shed on the cross for the forgiveness of your sins and conviction over your ongoing sin against the One who died so you could be freed from the power and influence of sin?

In some parts of Africa and Asia people travel hours by foot just to get to church and then hours to return home. In between, they spend four to six hours hearing God's Word and worshiping Him in spirit and in truth. In spite of having far less than we have in America, they exhibit the peace and joy of the Holy Spirit in true Christian fellowship. And, by the way, in some of those nations their very lives are in danger by attending Christian fellowship.

It is time for a reality check. Do you worship God with your lips while your heart is far from Him (Isaiah 29:13)? By the way, look at what God says are the *effects* of this in verse 14-16:

> *"Therefore, behold, I will again do wonderful things with this people, with wonder upon wonder; and the wisdom of their wise men shall perish, and the discernment of their discerning men shall be hidden." Ah, you who hide deep from the*

Lord your counsel, whose deeds are in the dark, and who say, "Who sees us? Who knows us?" You turn things upside down! Shall the potter be regarded as the clay, that the thing made should say of its maker, "He did not make me"; or the thing formed say of him who formed it, "He has no understanding"? (Isaiah 29:14-16)

This is what is happening in American Christianity! It has become an evil institution in God's eyes because the toxic combination of fake worship and human leadership (rather than God's leadership) are feeding each other on their journey to becoming Babylon. This toxic combination of fake worship and human leaders being elevated to the level of God produce these effects:

- Wisdom will perish.

- Discernment will be hidden.

- Things are turned upside down from God's Word.

- The clay starts to think of itself as greater than the potter who forms it.

Because of wisdom perishing, discernment being hidden, and the clay starting to elevate itself to the level of the potter, American Christianity is unable to see the grievous error of her ways and she thinks she is serving God. Instead, she is starting to align with Antichrist. And those who fall for her seductive deceptions will follow her blindly to eternal destruction as part of Babylon.

The next time you hear the alarming statistics of young people leaving the Christian faith you can blame government, media, or public education if you want. Or you can embrace the reality of the situation: they are leaving because American Christianity offers them no truthful answers to their serious questions. It's time for the church to stop acting like the old person wearing the bad hair piece, undergoing excessive plastic surgery, or dressing like someone from the disco era to look hip. It is time to start acting like mature adults, answering the serious questions our young people have, and mentoring them in the ways and wisdom of the One who created them, loves them, and wants to rescue them from hopelessness.

If you are in an American Christianity church you are part of the problem, not part of the solution. Once you realize this you are faced with a choice: Do you stay in your church for a while and try to influence your leadership to abandon the deception they have fallen under? Or do you walk away and join a Biblical church immediately?

Chapter Nine

Should I Stay or Should I Go?

This book gives you the information and tools from God's Word to discern if the church you belong to is trending toward becoming more of a Biblical Christian church or headed in the opposite direction of a church that is following man and is perhaps one step away from one day worshiping the ultimate man: Antichrist. But the decision to leave a church you have invested in and attended for years is not an easy one, and it shouldn't be. No person or institution is always right; none are above corruption and straying from God's standards. There are churches which have been awakened to a dangerous drift and have corrected those drifts, coming back to Biblical Christianity. Others started off as solid Biblical churches but have been slowly seduced into humanism by the father of lies and his influence on the worldly institutions he controls. If your church is headed in the wrong direction, we must uncover the real agenda of the church's leadership to determine if they are *deceivers* or are simply *being deceived*.

None of us is beyond deception. But a humble person, when confronted with the deception influencing them, will acknowledge their errors when confronted with truth; and only God can speak real truth, so the Bible must be the sole method of judgment. On the other hand, a *deceiver* will seek to justify or excuse his error because his agenda is more important to him than pursuing truth. He might claim to believe the Word of God is inerrant truth but will dismiss its clear teachings and warnings as "misinterpreted." And here is where American Christianity has successfully duped its followers. It has used flawed human understanding to interpret the Word of God instead of using the Bible as the sole means to interpret itself. And because we have become so preoccupied with the pursuit of wealth, comfort, and entertainment through television and social media, we fall into the trap of letting flawed humans interpret the perfection of God's Word because we are too lazy to take the time to study it deeply. We consume the "bread" of this world instead of the eternal Bread of Life.

Before a decision can be reached on whether to stay or leave a church, we need to be humble and graceful enough to not assume that church leadership is *intentionally* leading the church astray. We must give them the opportunity to recognize their errors and correct them.

Understand one basic fact: Every church wants to grow in numbers, and it should want that. Ultimately, church growth, in one form or another, is the goal of every church. The Biblical Christian church wants growth in numbers so more will come to saving faith in the full gospel and be transformed into holiness by the power of God's Word and Spirit. American Christian churches want growth to expand budgets and develop more man-made programs. Acts 2 shows that God is the cause of *real* Christian growth (numbers and depth). American Christianity believes *man* is the cause of church growth. It is focused only on numbers, not true spiritual growth and maturity. So discovering *why* your church wants to grow will help you determine if its true agenda is godly or humanist.

Uncovering the real agenda of church growth is a two-step process:

- What do church leaders believe the cause of church growth is: God or clever human programs and methods?

- Who did Jesus establish His church for? Saints or unrepentant sinners?

Discovering what church leaders perceive as the cause and effects of church growth helps every other disagreement come into correct focus. Once you can recognize whether your church is depending on God or on their own human understanding to grow the church, along with their understanding of what church membership is supposed to be, you will find that their doctrinal beliefs will eventually line up to support their mission: the nature and character of God, how we define the gospel, salvation and sanctification, the role and structure of the church, and how Christians navigate life as born-again believers with the remnants of our sinful nature still within us (desire for sanctification instead of embracing "cheap grace"). When we follow the doctrines in God's Word, *He* will be the cause for church growth and the effects will be a spiritually healthy and maturing fellowship. But if we teach the doctrines of men over God, *man* is the cause of church growth and to maintain and expand that growth more and more, man-made doctrine will have to replace the Bible. Eventually, a church doing this will have so little biblical doctrine and so much man-made doctrine that it will follow and serve Antichrist instead of Jesus Christ in the final days.

The "Statement of Faith or Beliefs" Deception

Here is the statement of beliefs from a large denomination:

> We believe in God, the Eternal Spirit, who is made known to us in Jesus our brother, and to whose deeds we testify:

> God calls the worlds into being, creates humankind in the divine image, and sets before us the ways of life and death. God seeks in holy love to save all people from aimlessness and sin. God judges all humanity and all nations by that will of righteousness declared through prophets and apostles.

> In Jesus Christ, the man of Nazareth, our crucified and risen Lord, God has come to us and shared our common lot, conquering sin and death and reconciling the whole creation to its Creator. God bestows upon us the Holy Spirit, creating and renewing the church of Jesus Christ, binding in covenant faithful people of all ages, tongues, and races.

> God calls us into the church to accept the cost and joy

of discipleship, to be servants in the service of the whole human family, to proclaim the gospel to all the world and resist the powers of evil, to share in Christ's baptism and eat at his table, to join him in his passion and victory.

God promises to all who trust in the gospel forgiveness of sins and fullness of grace, courage in the struggle for justice and peace, the presence of the Holy Spirit in trial and rejoicing, and eternal life in that kingdom which has no end.

It acknowledges belief in God and in Jesus as Savior and Lord. It calls us to the "joy of discipleship." It states that all who "trust in the gospel" receive God's grace and are forgiven. So what could be wrong? Maybe you have found that wonderful Biblical Christian church? But dig a little deeper into this denomination's website and you find this:

"Open and Affirming [("ONA")] is a journey of building inclusive churches and other ministry settings that welcome the full participation of LGBT people in the UCC's life and ministry. Please note: Many UCC congregations which may not have adopted an ONA covenant for various reasons are nevertheless welcoming and safe communities for gay, lesbian, bisexual, and transgender Christians."

Under their "justice" section you will find no mention of the murder of innocent children by abortion. You will find appeals to embrace LGBTQ as acceptable and pleasing in God's eyes, promotion of a united world government, and passionate pleas to embrace the climate change agenda. Also, while the "gospel" is mentioned, notice there is no definition of it and no reference whatsoever to the Bible's authenticity or authoritativeness.

This is a classic example of a church that denies the nature and character of God while claiming to embrace it. An example of man-made doctrine replacing biblical doctrine. And unless you can spot clever deception it will draw you into human worship instead of God worship; and then you are only one step away from one day worshiping Antichrist himself.

Unless you take the time to go through a statement of faith or beliefs, and are able to ask specific questions and request exact definitions of words from those who wrote it, you can be easily deceived. There are a growing number of Christian denominations and churches that have nice-sounding statements of faith, but when you drill down a little and see what they actually teach, it is obvious that even they do not believe their own statement of faith. Is this conscious deception or is it done out of ignorance of God's Word?

One of the more intriguing situations is when they state that they believe the Bible is inerrant truth yet support a doctrine that contradicts the Bible itself. They will make the argument that it is a "matter of interpretation." That is a red herring, deflecting from a principle that every serious Christian must understand: *The Bible is the sole instrument that must be used to accurately interpret itself since it is the only source of truth.* When we understand non-contradiction and how God never contradicts Himself, we begin to understand that the only area of confusion in Bible interpretation is our own human shortages in understanding God. And it is perfectly fine to admit that we do not fully understand the more subtle doctrines in God's Word, like those that talk of conviction of our consciences. But to claim to believe that the Bible is the Word of God, and then claim that it contradicts itself is an attack on the very nature and character of God Himself. And when we do not get His nature and character correct, we cannot get anything correct.

So in a world of confusion and deception, a world that is training us to abandon rational thought for feelings, a world that is redefining the very definitions God has given for His own words, how can we know that a church or denomination's statement of faith is actually consistent with the Bible? It will explain the terminology and words used by clearly defining them. I can tell you, "I believe in God," but you still do not know which "God" I believe in. I can tell you, "I believe in Jesus Christ," but you still don't know *what* I believe about Him. Is He a great teacher or God in the flesh? I can tell you I'm a Christian because Jesus died on a cross for my sins, but still fail to be saved through heartfelt confession and repentance.

You believe that God is one; you do well. Even the demons believe—and shudder! (James 2:19)

If you have serious concerns that can be contextually confirmed by God's Word about the method for growth in your church, I would suggest the following:

- Ask for a private meeting with church leadership, and do not talk with others about your concerns before that. Gossip and falsely accusing a brother of sin are serious offenses against God. If you have a group of fellow Christians with the same concerns, meet as a group with church leadership and do not seek to "expand" the circle beforehand.

- When you meet with church leadership, explain your concerns, stating that you understand the real possibility that perhaps you are hearing or seeing something different from the intent of church leadership.

- Be specific and "big picture" about your concerns. Do not argue over relatively unimportant issues such as the style of worship music or the specific translation of the Bible that is being used.

- Be praying that God opens eyes to what the real issues are. Do not get sidetracked, but try to identify the *cause* and not just deal in *effects*. Is your concern centered on crucial issues such as the nature and character of God, the presentation of a false or incomplete gospel, the mission of the church (Jesus' Great Commission or a human mission), or teaching only the benefits of salvation while ignoring the responsibilities of it (pursuing holy living)? Or is it a battle not worth fighting and something that falls under "matters of conscience" that Paul taught on?

- Always and only use God's Word with His words and definitions as the arbitrator of any disagreements. Remember there is only one correct interpretation of the Scriptures: The one God intended.

- A question you can ask is this: If God said you could have either a larger church that is spiritually less mature or a smaller church with committed disciples of Jesus, which would you choose? (Do not let them cop out with a "large church with strong disciples" answer.) Their answer might give you an indication of which type of church growth they truly value – God's or man's.

If you are convinced your church is selling out to American Christianity, pray fervently and ask God if you should stay a little longer, trying to be an instrument of godly change, or leave the church immediately and find a Biblical Christian church. I have friends who I believe are truly born-again believers who choose to remain in the Catholic Church in spite of serious concerns over the sexual abuse scandals rocking the church, along with Catholic doctrines like the status and role of Mary. They elect to stay there in order to, in their words, "be light and salt." Assuming that is not just a deceptive statement to cover up their fear of losing family or friends, I can respect their reasoning. But recently I came across something taught in the Roman Catholic Catechism I was unaware of concerning the nature and character of God, something few people including Catholics, know. This is directly from the Roman Catholic Catechism 841: *The Church's relationship with the Muslims.* "The plan of salvation also includes those who acknowledge the Creator, in the first place amongst whom are the Muslims; these profess to hold the faith of Abraham, and together with us they adore the one, merciful God, mankind's judge on the last day."

In my previous book, *American Christianity's Adultery with Secular Culture*, I document, using the Bible and the Qur'an, that Allah and God are not the same, and in fact they are completely contradictory in their nature and character. Can you stay in a church that believes Muslims worship the same God as Christians? And why is the Catholic Church not publicly open and transparent about that belief? This is a question I ask my Catholic friends because, as serious as the misinterpretations of Roman Catholicism are about Mary and other doctrines, the Muslim issue cuts to the very nature and character of God, and if you get that wrong you cannot get anything right nor know truth.

Why is the Catholic Church not openly transparent about this doctrine and teaching it to its members? Perhaps because they know if they did at this time they would lose members by the millions because of Muslim terrorism. But as fallen man becomes more and more evil by ignoring God's Word and listening to the deception of Satan with his growing control of worldly institutions, many will come to actually believe that Allah and God are one and the same, and then the stage is set for Antichrist to finally unite mankind by uniting the world's two largest religions, throwing aside divisive religious doctrines that hinder mankind from determining his own future.

If you are a Protestant or evangelical Christian you might be saying that we have to expose this Catholic doctrine so Catholics will come out of Babylon and join the true church! But you might be surprised to know that the very Protestant denomination or evangelical church you attend might believe the very same thing: that Muslims and Christians worship the same God. This is slowly being perpetuated by a deception many Christian leaders are falling for: calling Islam an "Abrahamic faith." Believing this deception plants the seeds for a fake human unity that is completely contradictory to the unity Jesus prayed for in His church (John 17). Rick Warren, Bill Hybels, and many other prominent leaders of American Christianity promote this deception. To study this in greater depth, please read *American Christianity's Adultery with Secular Culture.*

I hope you are beginning to understand how subtle and dangerous it is when a denomination or church starts replacing biblical doctrine with man-made doctrine, and when we follow men instead of Jesus Christ as our shepherd. Eventually this will lead to worshiping Antichrist, the ultimate man of charisma, charm, and persuasion. And once you pledge your allegiance to him through the mark of the beast, the Bible says you are permanently doomed to eternal damnation.

If your church or denomination is headed in the wrong direction, away from the Word of God instead of pressing into it, and when confronted in their error they defend their position and pull rank on you by citing the requirement to obey and honor them because they are "God's anointed," run from that church as fast as you can and find a church that is committed to God and His Word instead of man. But always make sure you give your church leaders a fair and honest opportunity to see their error and humble themselves before God.

One more thing that will probably get you out of your comfort zone and that goes against the way we are being conditioned as American Christians is *do not leave quietly*. Tell your family, friends, and church members why you must leave that church. Do not be badgered, intimidated, or threatened into silence. Do not allow yourself to become an instrument for the destruction of souls by downplaying your reason for leaving a church that is committed to following man instead of God. Do not rant and rave about your reasons for leaving; do it calmly, rationally, and truthfully. But I will warn you what might happen, because it has happened to me in the eight years of doing *Stand Up For the Truth* radio and exposing the dangerous path of American Christianity: You will lose friends. You need to decide if Jesus Christ is worth losing friends and even family members.

> *"Do not think that I have come to bring peace to the earth. I have not come to bring peace, but a sword. For I have come to set a man against his father, and a daughter against her mother, and a daughter-in-law against her mother-in-law. And a person's enemies will be those of his own household. Whoever loves father or mother more than me is not worthy of me, and whoever loves son or daughter more than me is not worthy of me. And whoever does not take his cross and follow me is not worthy of me. Whoever finds his life will lose it, and whoever loses his life for my sake will find it."* (Matthew 10:34-39)

Summary

Leaving a church you have attended for years is not an easy thing, and it shouldn't be. Too often people leave churches for the wrong reasons over petty squabbles or minor differences. But the growing apostasy in American Christianity cannot be ignored, and it is reaching a point where it is becoming the exact opposite of what Jesus desires of His true church. The subtle changes introduced slowly over time are not easily detectable, but they have an accumulative effect as we become used to following the direction and teachings of man instead of God. It starts with one person of influence – a pastor, elder, or church member – introducing doctrines or directives that contradict God's Word. Left unchallenged (because American Christianity promotes human unity over truth), it becomes a subtle movement that undermines God's Word, following men instead of God. And I will hammer on this nail until it is fully understood: When we decide to follow man instead of God, we are one step away from following the most charismatic, eloquent man ever born – Antichrist.

If you decide to leave your American Christian church you may be called a divider, judgmental, a Sanballat, an instigator, or unloving. You may lose friends. Is all that worth it to hear the King of Kings and Lord of Lords say to you, "Well done, good and faithful servant" when you stand before Him?

> *For what does it profit a man if he gains the whole world and loses or forfeits himself? For whoever is ashamed of me and of my words, of him will the Son of Man be ashamed when he comes in his glory and the glory of the Father and of the holy angels.* (Luke 9:25-26)

> *"The one who rejects me and does not receive my words has a judge; the word that I have spoken will judge him on the last day."* (John 12:48)

It is the Word of Jesus Christ, not the words of men, that will be used to judge us on the day of the Lord. That judgment is final and there cannot be any appeal to a higher court. The excuse of, "But my pastor or the television preacher misled me" will be rebuked because we have God's Word available to us. American Christianity has sold out to the world, and every day you remain in it you risk becoming entrenched in it to the point that it starts to feel right. This is because it is feeding our flesh and our sinful nature. Come out of Babylon before you become part of Babylon.

Chapter Ten

The Benefits of a Biblical Christian Church

There are still some solid Biblical Christian churches in our nation. And if you know how to spot them and you are truly committed to becoming a disciple of Jesus Christ, you will find great joy and comfort when you become a part of one. You will find yourself growing in the knowledge and grace of Jesus Christ (2 Peter 3:18). Because the Word of God is taken seriously and studied in-depth you will rediscover your "first love" (Revelation 2:4). The passion and commitment you first experienced when you became born again will be reignited and you will seek God with all your heart, mind, and strength.

You will have a passion to share the gospel with family and friends by speaking the truth with love and grace. The Holy Spirit within you will help you take your thoughts captive in obedience to Christ (2 Corinthians 10:5). You will receive the mind of Christ (1 Corinthians 2:16). You will cross a beautiful line in your relationship with God, from compliance to commitment. No longer will you strive with your human strength and understanding to find joy and peace. You will enter the Sabbath rest God wants you to experience (Hebrews 4:9-10): a place where worshiping God and obeying Him become natural and the positive effects are felt every day.

Your prayer life will cease to be some rote form of one-way conversation with God where you ask and strive to hear a response but are left frustrated thinking that God does not care. He will answer you by pointing you to His Word in a powerful way. Once you know and understand the Scriptures, they will come alive and God's Spirit will point you to the ones that answer your prayers.

No longer will going to church be an interruption or inconvenience; it will become a true joy. And no longer will church be something you *do* on Sunday; it will become who you *are* all week long as part of the body of Christ, cherished by Him and equipped to do His will.

A while back I was talking with two of our elders as we prepared for our time of fellowship and food right after our time of worship and hearing God's Word preached accurately and powerfully. I thanked them for their courage in stepping out in faith several years earlier in forming the fellowship after much prayer. I tried to put into words the vast depth of emotion I feel every time I hear God's Word taught at our fellowship. Here are the points I made to them:

- I realize my unrepentant sin and rebellion against God warranted my eternal damnation. I am ashamed of how I hated Him while He loved me.

- But I am filled with joy that He has redeemed me from sin and death.

- And then I experience a renewed passion to love and obey Him all the more because of how much He loves me and all He has spared me from. I realize He is even holier than I could understand, I am more sinful than I even realize, and yet He has redeemed me and wants to draw me closer to Himself so I can live a life of peace and joy.

- I cross the line from compliance to commitment in my journey to become a committed disciple of the One who rescued me.

- I leave the fellowship more committed than when I arrived that morning to love and obey God, to share the good news with family and friends, to pray more and rely more on

God and less on me, and to rest in His eternal Sabbath He has provided for me.

- I find the true and lasting peace of God that transcends all human understanding (Philippians 4:7). That peace is no longer an empty hope but a reality, allowing me to stand strong in the midst of a world that hates God and His adopted children more and more every day, and to love and pray for my enemies like Jesus did: *"Forgive them, for they know not what they do"* (Luke 23:34).

What are the lasting effects I enjoy from the gamut of emotions I experience within our fellowship?

- I am at complete peace knowing my sins, though they still are many, are forgiven, but I truly detest my ongoing sins and want to stop sinning because I love God.

- When I realize God is holier than I know, and my sin and rebellion against Him is deeper than I realize, it makes His grace all the more amazing. And I am committed to never invoking His grace as a license to go on sinning. I find true joy in pursuing holiness and perfection in Him, realizing it will only be attained when He completes His work in me and I stand before Him.

- I now look at the enemies of the gospel with compassion rather than anger, disgust, and pride. I realize the only thing that distinguishes their evil intent and actions from mine is the grace of God.

- My marriage with Nancy (now twenty-five years) is more joyful and rich every day. I love her more every day because I love God more every day. And she loves me more every day (in spite of my peculiarities) because she loves God more every day. She is more beautiful and pleasing to me with each passing day.

- I thoroughly enjoy the freedoms God has given me: good food, an occasional glass of beer, Milwaukee Brewers baseball, my work in the ministry, and the time spent with the phones off and doing nothing except relaxing. But I also will not allow them to become my "master"; I find the biblical conjunctive where freedoms and responsibilities or restrictions come together in truth.

- I look forward to the day when Jesus returns or takes me home without obsessing over it and becoming useless for Him while I am still in this life. I study His prophecies without obsessing over them. I embrace the mission and purpose He has given me as part of His church in Matthew 28:19-20.

- I experience spirited yet loving discussions with fellow believers about doctrines we interpret differently because we are both pursuing truth instead of trying to prove we are right. This helps us to interpret God's Word more accurately and experience joy if a brother can prove to me I was wrong because I have grown in the knowledge and grace of Jesus.

If you are not experiencing these effects in your life, would you like to? Finding and actively participating in a true Christian fellowship that teaches the full counsel of God's Word and understands exactly what Christian fellowship is according to the Bible will bring you peace and joy. But finding such a fellowship is not easy because we have been manipulated and conditioned to accept church as it *is* rather than what it *should be.* American Christianity has conditioned us to accept the scraps that fall from the table instead of pulling up a chair to the great feast Jesus has prepared for us. American Christianity wants you to remain in a state of confusion and dependence upon it instead of being totally dependent on God, because if we rely on God, then American Christianity is no longer needed. And if it is no longer needed, all the bloated budgets and manufactured careers go away.

American Christianity churches use subtle deception to make people believe they are following Jesus when in reality they are trying to replace Him as leader. Some do it consciously and purposefully while others are doing it unconsciously and out of ignorance. Both are wrong and have no place in Jesus' true church.

In the previous chapter we discovered a deceptive statement of beliefs from a prominent American Christianity church. I would propose the following template as a starting point to a meaningful and biblical statement of faith or beliefs, and allowing God to develop a strong, faithful Christian fellowship:

> We believe and trust in God's nature and character as He has revealed in His Word: He is always righteous and eternally just. All of His actions (love, compassion, grace, and judgment) come from His eternally righteous and just nature.

> We believe the Bible is God's revelation about Himself and all His creation. We believe the only correct interpretation of the Bible is understood by allowing the Bible to interpret itself in a non-contradictory manner since God is non-contradictory. Since only God is always right, and every man or institution is some combination of right and wrong, any attempt to interpret God's Word with human understanding is futile and ultimately leads us further from God rather than drawing us nearer to Him.

> Truth only comes from God. Since man is imperfect and cannot know all things past, present, and future, he cannot be a source for truth since all information required has not yet been revealed. Thus, we trust in God's Word as our only source for truth and test all our human opinions and theories against it.

> We believe sinful man is saved solely by the grace of God through complete faith and trust in who Jesus Christ is and what He accomplished through His death, burial, and resurrection according to the Bible. We believe the gospel of salvation is that of a perfect God reconciling sinful man

back to a righteous standing before Him. The gospel contains these necessary components:

- Man recognizing his wretched, sinful rebellion against God, confessing it before God in heartfelt prayer

- Repenting of our sinful beliefs and actions, consciously recognizing that our sins are a grave affront to God, and being committed to walking away from our sinful desires and to becoming sanctified by God's grace

- Placing our complete faith and trust in Jesus Christ alone as the only sufficient sacrifice to God who can permanently forgive our sins and reconcile us to God as righteous

- Trusting in God, through His Word and Spirit, to begin to purify our conscience and be transformed into the image of Jesus Christ

We are committed to loving God with all our mind, heart, and strength. We gather in Christian fellowship to encourage and when necessary lovingly rebuke one another when our beliefs, words, and actions do not line up with our commitment.

We believe what the Bible teaches about the final return of Jesus Christ to judge all men according to His Word. Those saved by God's grace will join Him in eternal life. Those outside of God's grace will be condemned to hell for eternity. There is no second chance available to those who die outside of God's grace.

We utilize church discipline as taught and applied in the Bible. If there is unresolved conflict between Biblical Christians, or a member is consciously living in unrepentant sin, we will make a judgment solely based on the Bible's teaching and application.

We are committed to loving one another as we love ourselves. We will help and encourage one another when life's challenges arise. We will speak the truth in love to one another to encourage and when necessary correct one another, always with complete truth and grace from God's Word. We are committed to one another to cooperate with God's Spirit in each of us to help us become part of Jesus' eternal and spotless bride.

We believe we are called to love and respect all human beings because they were created by God in His image. While we might reject their worldview, belief system, or lifestyle, we respect their human dignity and love them enough to share the truth of God and the eternal destiny of every soul with them.

We commit to sharing the gospel with those we know and meet, always speaking the truth with real love and a desire to welcome more people as adopted sons and daughters of God through the gospel of reconciliation.

We gather regularly to hear and understand the Word of God, glorify Him, share as needs arise, and celebrate the sacrifice of Jesus Christ for the forgiveness of our sins.

We welcome individuals to visit our fellowship to hear the Word of God if they are truly seeking Him. But please understand that Christian fellowship is reserved solely for people who become born-again believers who seek to become faithful, passionate disciples of Jesus Christ. After your first visit the member of our fellowship who invited you will meet with you and our church elders to answer any questions and explain the benefits and requirements of belonging to the fellowship. The requirement is that you accept and believe in the gospel of salvation described above, committing your life solely to Jesus Christ as Savior and Lord of your life. Once this is done, the fellowship becomes your family to guide and help you in pursuit of holy living.

We recognize that every man, even the truly born-again believer, will continue to struggle with temptation and occasional sin. The fellowship is here to encourage, teach, and when necessary correct born-again believers when our words and actions do not reflect what God's Word teaches about how true believers should live. This will always be done by speaking the truth in true Christian love and grace. The fellowship understands we are far from perfect, but seeks to be perfected by God's Word and Spirit. Repentant sinners struggling against temptation and sin are always welcome. Unrepentant sinners, consciously choosing to continually disobey God, are not welcome to be a part of the fellowship.

Once a statement of faith or beliefs is adopted, the fellowship should create documents that clearly state what they believe about specific issues and questions people might have. The fellowship should be very clear about what they believe about any issue or doctrine in question. This gives the elders and members a reference point to settle disputes and rightfully administer church discipline if warranted. And the documents should be expanded as new issues come into public discussion. Twenty years ago, who would have thought our nation would legalize homosexual marriage? Two years ago, who would have anticipated that gender dysphoria and fluidity would be defining issues in our nation? If we allow ambiguity or uncertainty to flourish, confusion and deception come knocking at our door. The true church of Jesus Christ has a responsibility to its members and the world to be clear about what we believe, why we believe it, and how our beliefs should lead us to interact with the world around us. To do less than that can open the door for the father of lies to whisper in our ears and sow seeds of deceit and contention.

The last point I want to make is sure to ruffle feathers and make people uncomfortable. *Consider going to a "zero-budget" fellowship with no paid staff or leaders.* Please know I am *not* saying that failure to do so is sinful or un-Christian, but the benefits of not being a slave to money or the financial laws of our nation are many. As the government's lust for more and more money to feed its greed and power increases, and the hatred of this world increases toward God, His Word, and His people, being freed from the yoke of money is a blessing. Know this: the very non-profit status that churches have become dependent upon to survive financially will be turned against them as a weapon to manipulate and control us one day. But if the fellowship is not a licensed non-profit entity and has no financial budget or dependence on givers, then it is unencumbered in teaching the truth. And Christians are then free to give generously as the Holy Spirit leads them, supporting God's work in our community and around the world.

The other important benefit is this: the zero budget system can prevent members of the church from following a man instead of God. A lack of need for money frees us up to preach the truth without compromise. No man is elevated as the sole teacher before the church; no single man is seen as the biblical authority. Instead, all members are encouraged to become serious students of the Bible, and a group of five to seven elders is much less likely to be seduced or deceived by the enemy than a single man. We are witnessing megachurches being built on the backs of a single man of eloquence and charisma – one step away from people worshiping Antichrist. Churches where pastors who are trained as CEOs are in charge instead of the church being entrusted to a group of qualified, dedicated elders as the Bible instructs, are churches headed toward serious trouble. Bill Hybels and Willow Creek Church, along with other examples of churches being corrupted by human ideals, are all around us. What will it take for Christians to wake up and see the effects of American Christianity all around us?

I realize this seems like a radical step that goes against everything we have been taught about church. But the fellowship we belong to has been successful with this model for several years. We see members stepping up to voluntarily support the fellowship with any costs and providing for the needs of one another generously. We see members being more generous in supporting God's work around the world because they are not being asked to support a building or a bloated church budget. This obviously requires elders who are qualified according to the Bible and passionate about shepherding those God has entrusted to them. It requires returning to the blueprint the Bible gives us for establishing and maintaining a true Biblical church.

Five-hundred years ago, Martin Luther confronted a church that had gone astray from God's Word, establishing a human institution where men were elevated and followed instead of God. It had come into an unholy alliance with government to suppress the truth and lead people into spiritual bondage. American Christianity is doing the same thing, and unless we come out of it, we can easily be deceived into following Antichrist one day while believing we are loving and serving God. That is how deceptive Satan is.

Jesus warned that many who think they are doing His work will be cast into eternal hell (Matthew 7). He also warned that false christs and prophets would arise who are so wondrous that even the elect will be deceived if possible (Matthew 24). It has been said that the measure of a man can be gauged by the friends he keeps. Similarly, the measure of a Christian might be gauged by the people he joins with in fellowship. Are we seeking a truly biblical unity that Jesus prayed for? Or a human unity built on shifting sand and relative truth? How your church handles biblical doctrine, including the character and nature of God, will give you the answer.

Final Thoughts

I realize this book is challenging and will shake many preconceived notions and beliefs to their core. That is because of something I teach people about their thought process when we are in discipleship development.

The Bible talks about four thought processes a man can utilize to establish his belief system, his standard of morality, and his subsequent decisions on important matters: evil, animal or fleshly, human, and godly. I will not go into great detail concerning them as I have already covered them extensively in *The Death of Christian Thought* published last year, except to say that true born-again believers are the only people who can use a godly thought process because we have received the Holy

Spirit. The best any unrepentant sinner can do is use a human thought process, which the Bible calls foolishness to God (1 Corinthians 3:19).

This verse points us to the one crucial thing we must understand if we are to see through the deception being perpetrated by American Christianity on unsuspecting people. We think of a human thought process as good, but not as good as a godly thought process. But a human thought process, according to the Bible, is the *opposite* of a godly thought process. Man at his core without God's Spirit is desperately wicked and foolish, and so are his thought processes and reasoning. American Christianity uses a human thought process to try to improve on God's ways and thoughts. This leads to the various and serious ills we see in different segments of American Christianity:

- Redefining God's nature and character in contradiction to His Word

- Believing *all* people go to heaven because of Jesus' sacrifice on the cross

- Confusing spiritual issues as political (abortion, homosexual marriage, and gender fluidity)

- Depending on the clever schemes of man to grow the church instead of relying on God

- A sinful human unity instead of a biblical unity built on the pursuit of spiritual purity and holiness

- Believing salvation is the end of the Christian journey instead of the impetus to being made holy by God's Word and Spirit

I could share stories I have heard from committed Christians about how they have been ostracized and belittled by elders for daring to respectfully question a doctrine being taught in the church; of elders being relieved of their positions for privately questioning the direction of the church in elder meetings; of church leaders insisting that the teachings of admitted apostates like Rob Bell and Brian McLaren be inserted into Bible studies; and of pastors who have been fired because their sermons didn't help the congregation feel better about their sinful lives they lead while claiming to be born-again believers. This is the status quo within American Christianity, and like the difference between the human and the godly thought processes, American Christianity has become the exact *opposite* of Biblical Christianity. God gave Ezekiel a calling and a warning:

> *"Son of man, I have made you a watchman for the house of Israel. Whenever you hear a word from my mouth, you shall give them warning from me. If I say to the wicked, 'You shall surely die,' and you give him no warning, nor speak to warn the wicked from his wicked way, in order to save his life, that wicked person shall die for his iniquity, but his blood I will require at your hand. But if you warn the wicked, and he does not turn from his wickedness, or from his wicked way, he shall die for his iniquity, but you will have delivered your soul. Again, if a righteous person turns from his righteousness and commits injustice, and I lay a stumbling block before him, he shall die. Because you have not warned him, he shall die for his sin, and his righteous deeds that he has done shall not be remembered, but his blood I will require at your hand. But if you warn the righteous person not to sin, and he does not sin, he shall surely live, because he took warning, and you will have delivered your soul."* (Ezekiel 3:17-21)

American Christianity ignores these verses because they are in the Old Testament, and if you ask about them, they will explain them away as only applying to Israel. That is a human thought process of picking and choosing what *they* think is important instead of just teaching what God has said. This calling and warning for Ezekiel is also a calling and warning for all Christians to be faithful watchmen on the wall to warn people of their transgressions against a holy God and the punishment that awaits them if they do not heed the warning, along with the judgment that awaits *us* if we do not warn them to begin with.

God's Word has warned us. If you have the Holy Spirit and study God's Word to take everything I have shared and hold it up against the Bible to measure its truth, I believe you will see what is happening around us and leave American Christianity for the true church of Jesus Christ. But the choice is yours because God has given you a free will.

> *And if it is evil in your eyes to serve the LORD, choose this day whom you will serve, whether the gods your fathers served in the region beyond the River, or the gods of the Amorites in whose land you dwell. But as for me and my house, we will serve the LORD.* (Joshua 24:15)

Choose this very day whom you will serve: The God of the Bible or the gods of American Christianity. But choose wisely because the consequences are eternal. One day, perhaps in our lifetime, one whom the Bible calls Antichrist will arrive on the scene. He will be the most charismatic, influential, and devious man the world has ever known. The world will exalt him above all other men, believing he has the answers to all our problems.

And if you are being conditioned by American Christianity to follow men instead of God, you will probably fall for his clever deception and end up worshiping Satan instead of God. If you are living in denial of that possibility, you have probably already been infected by American Christianity, and unless you remove this cancer it will grow and fester.

Work from within to try to return American Christianity to Biblical Christianity if you feel called to do so. But be careful, because it is so deceptive that you could be seduced by it, and it will not end well for your eternal soul. Better to leave a little early rather than too late, because Babylon's eternal fate has been sealed by God and all remaining in it will perish.

Speak the truth in love, always full of grace. But remember that love without truth is not love at all.

Meet the Author

M ike LeMay is an author, biblical apologist, radio talk show host, and general manager of Q90 FM, a Christian radio station in Green Bay, Wisconsin. He has extensively studied and reported on news, issues, and trends pertaining to the Christian life, pointing people to the truth of God's Word.

His books have received critical acclaim for their insight in bringing news and topics of the day into correct biblical context and understanding, helping Christians see the big picture of what is happening around them. His latest book, American Christianity's Slide into Apostasy: What We Must Do before It's Too Late, points out the growing disparity between Biblical Christianity and an "American Christianity" that is integrating secular beliefs, thoughts, and processes into the church, leading people further away from God and His eternal truth.

Mike is also owner of Christian Thought Consulting, LLC, and he helps families and business professionals find peace, joy, and purpose in their increasingly busy lives. He can be reached at 920-676-7083 or www.michaeldlemay.com.

Visit Michael online at:

www.michaeldlemay.com

Also by Michael D. LeMay

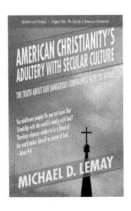

**American Christianity's Adultery with
Secular Culture, by Michael D. LeMay**

**An honest look at where the church in America is headed and what
we can do to change course.**

American Christianity is dying a slow death at its own hands. Instead of
positively affecting the secular culture, we are being infected by it under
the guise of being "seeker-friendly" and "loving." Soon, the church may
be an exact mirror of the culture that seeks to destroy us. With a lack
of strong, principled leaders, and with followers who want their ears
tickled instead of being challenged to pursue righteousness, American
Christianity is writing its own epitaph as it slowly dies.

Unless we reverse course by embracing the complete, absolute truth
of God's Word and stop trying to redefine God in our selfish human
image, only a remnant will remain of a once-powerful church. Do we
have the courage to challenge ourselves and our leaders to reject secular
culture and its influences? Or will we continue to die a slow death at
our own hands as we continue to inhale the cancer of secular humanism? Time is running out.

Original Title: The Suicide of American Christianity

Available where books are sold

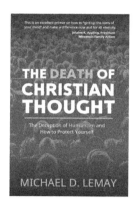

The Death of Christian Thought, by Michael D. LeMay

We are being lied to—and many professing Christians are buying the lies. Your eternal soul may be at stake. The Bible foretells a great deception and falling away from the faith in the latter days where absolute truth is discounted and moral relativism is elevated: Humanism!

The clever deception of Humanism has completely taken over government, media and public education, and has infiltrated the visible church so strongly that many churches differ little in their beliefs and teachings from the humanist views of the world.

This book will open your eyes to the rampant deception around us and help you correctly interpret the Word of God so you can stand strong in your faith to the end. It will help you open the eyes of family and friends who fall for the deception of Humanism, and point them to the eternal hope of Jesus Christ. It will teach you how to take your thoughts captive in obedience to Christ and live a life of joy, peace and obedience to God.

You will see how God designed our brain, heart and conscience to work, and how the truth of the Bible and the Holy Spirit can help you live a life of joy and peace as the world continues to spin out of control.

Available where books are sold

Are You Really Saved? by Michael D. LeMay

"Are You Really Saved?" is a book that will challenge everything you think you know about God, eternal life and hell. Far too many professing Christians cannot explain why they believe what they claim to believe, relying on others to explain the teachings of God. Jesus Christ is very clear that the path to eternal life with God is very narrow, and few people find it. Yet most professing Christians do not think twice about these words of Jesus. They think because they were baptized as a baby, or attend a certain church, that they are destined for eternal life in heaven. But the Bible tells a much different story. Jesus said unless we love Him with all our heart, mind and strength, we will not enter eternall life with Him. Yet most professing Christians know more about their favorite sport team or television show than they do the teachings of the One who came to save us. This book will challenge you to the very essence of your soul.

Available where books are sold

Also by the publisher

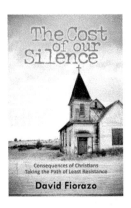

The Cost of Our Silence, by David Fiorazo

There are consequences when God's people take the path of least resistance and back out of culture. One only needs to look at our society to see we are living with those consequences today.

- Why do you think so many Christians pursue comfort over commitment to Christ?

- Do you sometimes feel overwhelmed by the darkness and moral decline in society today and wonder what happened to the salt and light?

- How have we reached a point where Christians who do preach the gospel and speak up about sin are called hateful, intolerant, or judgmental?

Christian in name only, America has become an epicenter for the culture war as too many of us keep ducking the issue of sin. Due to decades of Christians being silent, failing to preach the gospel and speak the truth in love, we've reached a tipping point in which political correctness refuses to coexist with religious freedom. Why do you think Christians who defend God's Word are often called hateful, intolerant, or judgmental? There are consequences in this life and for eternity, when Christians take the path of least resistance. We cannot reverse the moral decline, but we can choose to stand for righteousness as we pray for revival and be the salt and light Jesus called us to be while we're still here.

Available where books are sold

Redefining Truth, by David Fiorazo

We now live in a culture that has embraced moral relativism, a generation that no longer believes truth can be known. Right and wrong, good and evil are measured by feelings and opinions. It is all part of a satanic delusion and much is at stake. Redefining Truth provides answers and biblical perspective to the most pressing issues in today's postmodern society.

Practically everything in life changes, but if God never changes and if absolute truth exists, then this investigation matters tremendously. You will be informed as we evaluate the overwhelming evidence supporting Christianity. You'll also be encouraged to cultivate an eternal perspective even as attacks on believers are increasing. Redefining Truth will show you how to respond to others in a loving and confident way. This book will also help you successfully navigate through the noise, agendas, distractions, and confusion prevalent in America today. It will give you facts, history, and Scripture you can use to answer skeptics and challenge others to consider the truth of Jesus Christ. No decision is more critical.

Available where books are sold

Eradicate, Blotting Out God in America
by David Fiorazo

Enemy forces continue to destroy this nation by attacking America's Judeo-Christian roots from within. This book will investigate government, media, Hollywood, public schools, our culture of death, and the push toward socialism and Marxism. You'll see how some churches and leaders are diluting the Word of God weakening the witness of believers. You may be outraged as this book exposes how sin is being openly promoted, yet encouraged because God is still in control. There's a remnant of committed Christians resisting evil and standing in the way. The choice is ours: who or what will we give our allegiance to, God or man; to Jesus Christ or to culture and politics? As Christians, our loyalties must not be divided any longer or America may be lost.

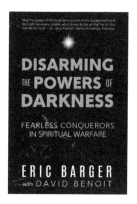

Disarming the Powers of Darkness, by Eric Barger

Scripture is clear: the spiritual battlefield is real and the Enemy is determined.

But most Christians are ill-equipped and unprepared when attacked, and even fewer are on the offensive. Still others write off spiritual warfare as irrelevant today, while on the other extreme some credit Satan for every imaginable problem in life. The purpose of this book is to provide biblical balance and clarity in order to establish a proper battle plan – exposing the Enemy for who he really is and showing Christians how to win this war with the spiritual weapons already at their disposal.

Available where books are sold

CPSIA information can be obtained
at www.ICGtesting.com
Printed in the USA
LVHW020838250219
608648LV00021B/253/P

9 781622 451029